I BLAMED YOU, YOU AND YOU

I BLAMED YOU, YOU AND YOU

The Lost and Found Kids

Johnny Richey

Transcribed & Edited by Muammar T. Adams

Copyright © 2021 by Johnny Richey.

All rights reserved. No part of this book may be reproduced in any form or by any electronic or mechanical means, including information storage and retrieval systems, without permission in writing from the publisher, except by reviewers, who may quote brief passages in a review.

ISBN: 978-1-956736-67-0 (Paperback Edition)
ISBN: 978-1-956736-68-7 (Hardcover Edition)
ISBN: 978-1-956736-66-3 (E-book Edition)

Book Ordering Information

Phone Number: 315 288-7939 ext. 1000 or 347-901-4920
Email: info@globalsummithouse.com
Global Summit House
www.globalsummithouse.com

Printed in the United States of America

Contents

Foreword-"Strengthening Your Kids, Young Men and Women to be Successful" 13
Introduction..15
A Dedication..17
Hi, my name is Shara 1
#1. Carrie 2
#2. Toya 4
#3. Maggie 6
#4. Little Tommy 8
#5. Dee-Dee 9
#6. Brendy 10
#7. Dariessa 11
#8. Monique 12
#9. Tia Tish – Girls Want Attention 13
#10. Mo Mo...14
#11. T. C. 15
#12. Warren – Gangs 16
#13. Danielle – Different People 17
#14. Shawn – Mother Dying.......................................18
#15. Audee..19
#16. Jeannie – White Girl 20
#17. Venus – Racism in School 21
#18. Rodisha – Drugs and Fighting.............................22
#19. Tyrone – Drugs and Gangs..................................23
#20. Rhoda – Mother Dying of Cancer.......................24
#21. Deborah - Talking About Meth 25
#22. Steva – Prostitution, Stealing and Cashing
     Stolen Checks 26
#23. Melva 27
#24. Tony – Stealing Money.......................................28
#25. Steve – Low Self-Esteem.....................................29

#26. Brandy - "He's Gay" 30
#27. La' Toya – She Was Ashamed.................................31
#28. Larry – Not a lot of Attention 32
#29. George – Talks About Food All the Time..................33
#30. Ronnie – The Color of HisSkin...............................34
#31. Shanrika - Joining Gangs..35
#32. Efforts 36
#33. Another Story about School Gangs.........................37
#34. Ernest – Pressured by Parents 38
#35. Eddie – A Christian Boy...39
#36. Demetria – Mother & Daughter Motivation Story....40
#37. Motivation 41
#38. Hakim – A Muslim's Story 42
#39. Salisha – She Killed Her Father & She
      Likes Women 43
#40. My name is Melvin..44
#41. Andy – Name Calling..45
#42. A Buddhist's Story 46
#43. Jeremiah – Gang Fight 47
#44. Dorisha – Girl BeingPicked-On 48
#45. Tanisha...49
#46. Debra – About Blocks 50
#47. Derrick..51
#48. Rita and Sita – Street Violence 52
#49. Shanisha – Self-Centered Girl 53
#50. Black Americans...54
#51. Melvin – A Boy That Likes Boys 55
#52. White Americans..56
#53. Ethiopian Americans 57
#54. Nalisha – Missing Little Girl 58
#55. Pleasure..59
#56. Doris – Whites Talking About Blacks 60
#57. Martell 61
#58. Larry 62
#59..63

#60. Sharon – About Black People 64
#61. "Success" 65
#62. Steve – About Blacks 67
#65. Darlene & Mr. Strickland: An Eating
		Disorder Story 69
#66. Teesha – Being Poor 70
#67. Bobby – White School 71
#68. Demo – Positive Thinking....................................72
#69. Ishira – Going to a Drug Program with her
		Mother..73
#70. Lilly – The Story Is About a Drug Baby..............74
#71. Darrin – Track and Field 75
#72. "My name is Ebony" - Homeless 76
#73. Oscar...77
#74. Lewis...78
#75. Donna – A Girl Acting Like a Boy 79
#76. Doris Monique...80
#77. Tammy...82
#78. Joy...83
#79. Dontae 84
#80. Hi, I'm Murray...85
#81. Jada...86
#82. Solisha – About Having a Boyfriend...................87
#83. Steve..88
#84. My name is Raymond 89
#85. Sandra..90
#86. The Story of Success: Purpose in Life..................91
#87. Larry...92
#88. Native Americans 93
#89. Donnie: If You Blame People................................94
#90. Hardy..95
#91. Demore 96
#92. C. Harty...97
#93. Steve..98
#94. Dennis – Another GangStory................................99

#95. Sheila 100
#96. Betty – Nothing Beats a Failure but a Try 101
#97. Learning to Give Your All..102
#98. Cause and Effect 103
#99. Loving Yourselves 104
#100. Desires 105
#101. Jean – Overweight...106
#102. The Good and The Bad 107
#103..108
#104. Maiya 109
#105. A Story of Two Women 110
#106. J. Ray – Another Gang Story..................................111
#107. Benisha – Crack Baby in a Foster Home...............112
#108. Stacy 113
#109. Fred..114
#110. O'dell 115
#111. Leroy: I Blame Some People for Blaming Others...117
#112. Tyler...119
#113. Irina 120
#114. Daijiro..121
#115. Sancis 122
#116. Kiki 123
#117. Kamilah 124
#118. Anthony – About Gangs 125
#119. Sandra..126
#120. Larry Roy 127
#121. De'Osha...128
#122. I Am You...129
#123. P. J..130
#124. Brenz..131
#125. Carrie 132
#126. Rosella..133
#127. Shanoshia 134
#128. Penny 135
#129. Niki..136

#130. Lee Lee 137
#131. Rayshawn 138
#132. Mohammed 139
#133. 140
#134. Adat 141
#135. Hi, I am You 142
#136. Emily - "We Are Americans" 143
#137. Jean – Adoption Story 144
#138. Hispanic Americans 145
#139. Norman – Another Gang Story 146
#140. Jewish Americans 147
#141. Mercy 148
#142. All Americans 149
#143. Sharon - A Ghetto Story 150
#144. Carolyn 151
#145. Seeing Your Own Reflection While You Create 152
Final Wisdom 153
Active Behavioral Conduct Disciplines© by Thomas Boothe ©1979 153
Final Wisdom 154
Boothe Protocol for Determining Ongoing Success 156

*Let your dominant thoughts prevail
and you will appear there!
Control your destiny.
Whatever you think
that's what you'll become.*

Foreword-"Strengthening Your Kids, Young Men and Women to be Successful"

In all cultures great leaders have arose and great results have happened. Some fought for human rights; some fought for freedom; and some fought for equality and independence. Integration is key to unity, happiness and peace. If we don't have unity, we are divided. We are the descendants of great people and nations! We are the children of prosperity and life! We are all "The Family Tree of Humanity". You might choose life but not prosperity! You might choose prosperity and not life! But what we can choose is to be around like-minded people who have chosen to do the right things in life; doing what the great men and women have done before us! We must lift each other up while lifting-up ourselves. That's what these great people did who came before you.

Introduction

Growing-up, I saw a lot of problems in the streets and schools; while going to school and coming from school. In big cities, I know students live rougher than smaller cities. It's hard for 7th and 8th graders and teens to overcome some of the peer pressures they face. I'm a witness to these pressures: drugs, sex, gangs and unstable homes, these are the norm. Even now it's hard to overcome thesechallenges that kids face today. To overcome as you grow up and realize there's no future for losers(you stop and think, Where am I going? Where will I be in 5 years? Will I graduate fromschool? Am I going to college? How am I being affected by my surroundings? What can I do and what will I do to change my course from failure to success? I didn't know how short life was untilnow.

A Dedication

This book goes out to all the kids that didn't get a chance to be loved or made to feel their stories were not important or their lives werenot significant. Maybe somewhere in these pages parts of your story may be heard and maybe then, you can finally feel complete in knowing not only that there's nothing wrong with you but you are not alone. My book is dedicated to the memories of parents who have lost their children to the streets, to drugs and to gangs.

-Johnny Richey

Hi, my name is Shara

I met this nice guy on the Internet. I'm 13 years old. He's 15 years old. We talk all the time. I gave him my phone number, we text each other every day and talk on the Internet. It's been 4 months now. I really like him. He said his name was J. B. You know, like Jeffery Beavers. Sometimes he says, "You look pretty today". I said, "How do you know?" He said, "I saw you today at school." Every now and then, J. B. would check on me. I felt sad, my dad left when I was 5 years old. One day J. B. texted me and asked me to skip school with him and meet at his parents' house. I said, "I don't know about that. My mother might find out." He said, "It will be our little secret." It was on a Thursday when I skipped school to go and see J. B. I went to his address, he gave me, about 3 miles from my school. I knocked on the door and an older man answered the door. I knew I was in trouble. I thought it was J. B.'s dad. He said, "Come in Felicia." I said, "How do you know my name? Where is J. B.?" He said, "I'm J. B." I was so scared. I said, "You're not 15 years old!" I walked right out of that house. This guy was old enough to be my father and that day I learned a very important lesson: Never Trust People on the Internet. They will tell you what you wanna' hear. He tricked me. I'm so happy I made it out of his house safe. and alive.

You will come face-to-face with grown-ups pretending they are kids. What would you do in that situation? Who would you tell? Don't be afraid to report these men and women pretending they are children or teenagers likeyou are. Tell on them, report them to teachers, parents or to your older brothers and sisters. What would you do?

#1. Carrie

My parents: they fought all the time about everything. Mostly money and dad cheating. Sometimes he would hit mom and she would fight back but daddy was too strong. I could heartheminthereoomsometimes, weonlyhada sheet over our door. Daddy drank all the time, he kept getting laid-off of his jobs. Sometimes mama would go to church and take us. It was sixofus, fourboysandtwogirls, andmamaand daddy made eight. We had a three bedroom apartment right in the worst part of town: the ghetto. We slept on the floors and I remember those little rats or mice running around. Insects, roaches. As we grew up I can remember going to school, watching people in the class, and one time the teacher said to me, "Carrie, stop daydreaming and picking your nose!" I was so embarrassed I felt like crying because others were laughing at me, so I didn't cry. I was inthe 6th grade. I was only 11 years old. All the fighting I saw and the fights, this has a lot to do with who I am today. You know, somethings just never leave; some things you never forget. I never forget the fights ofmy parents, my friends, and the things I heard in church. It seems like I was caught between hell and heaven, good and bad, right and wrong. My mother worked all the time, my grandmother watched us a lot and she came over just to sit with us. My mother's mother was so kind and sweet I really loved her. My grandfather is dead, he died before I was born. If it wasn't for my parents fighting all the time, and if they would have paid more attention to me, I would not have gotten pregnant atthe age of 14 years old and would've finished school. Yes I got a job, I've been on welfare for 15 years.

I BLAMED YOU, YOU AND YOU

Now I work at Burger King. I've been there for 15 years. I never went back to school because I don't have time, I am too busy raising babies and looking for me a man to help me take care of my five babies. I blame all this on my mother andfather.

-Carrie

What does Carrie see her life as?

#2. Toya

When I was in school they used to tell me, "don't be so sad". "Why you so mad all the time girl"? It's how I grew up, mama and daddy never had no money. I never had new clothes for school. Man, I looked like a tramp! All the clothes I had was used, Goodwill stuff. Stuff didn't nobody want but mama. I had two little sisters who got on my nerves. I had to get out of that house. My mother's boyfriend kept messing with me when she was at work. Grandma used drugs. I heard mama talking to her friends about a lot of stuff. The talk never ended. When Christmas came we never got nothing. Sometimes I would lie about some things we got for Christmas. I just made up some toys or whatever. I left when I was 13 years old. I got out of there. I met this guy, he was 19 years old. He liked me. He said I looked like I was about 18 or 19 years old. He made me feel good 'cause I wanted to look older. When I was 15 years old, he took me to this "After Hours" Club, 'cause I didn't need no I. D. to get in .I was pregnant by then, I wanted a baby. I never visited mama. But grandma, I saw her. I used to have a lot of money. Sometimes I would see grandma and give her10 or 15 dollars. I know what she did with it. But I didn't care. She told mama she saw me and I was working the streets but I don't care. I was out of that house. I know Drae loved me and that's all I needed. We stayed in motels for a while until we got our apartment. I stayed with Drae for 15 years working the streets. I got four kids, me and Drae broke-up. I still have that same apartment, still on welfare. Idropped-out of school in the 8th grade, if it wasn't for my mama's

I BLAMED YOU, YOU AND YOU

old boyfriend, I may have finished school... But I blame Stanley, my Mama's boyfriend.

-Toya

What should she have done?

#3. Maggie

My mother started me drinking when I was 10 years old. I was the only girl she had, my mother sold drugs. Her boyfriend had a lot of money. They bought me whatever I wanted. They had new cars, nice clothes and diamond rings. I walk to school all the time. One day some girls stopped me and my friend and tried to take my coat from me. It was five of them. We fought. And some older people walked-up and told them girls to leave us alone and go to school. If it wasn't for the old people, they would have got my coat and beat-us-down. I told my mother and that night she gave me a knife for protection. She said if it happened again, cut them. I said, "Okay" and took the knife. The next day I showed it to myfriend while walking to school. She wanted one too. One day going to school, or before I left, I had a drink. Mother didn't know I had some, but when I got to school, in my class one of the girls was in class and we fought right in the classroom. I was taken to the Principal's Office. They smelled the alcohol on my breath and called my mother. She had to come and get me, and they smelled alcohol on her breathtoo. C. S. D. (Child Services Division) was called after she and I left school and they came to the house. And, mama put them out. They called the police and mother had to send me to my grandmother, out-of-state, because she knew they would take me from her. So I started school in my new town in my grandmother's maiden name. Lucky it was the beginning of the year, mother had started me in another school, so they used the old records of the otherschool to enroll me out-of-state. I started missing my friends and my mother and I ran away from home. I was 11 years old. That night, the police picked me up and called my grandmother. And she came and got me. I don't like living with my grandmother 'cause I don't know her that well and my grandfather worked all thetime. But I knew I didn't want to stay there withthem. So I started stealing money out of her purse and drinking with older girls in the parkafter-school. And I was walking from the park back to grandmother's, and got hit by a car. I was in the hospital for almost 3 ½ months. My mother and boyfriend came down to help with me. Now I can't walk that good. I am a cripple and in pain, I love pills. I stay high. I blame mymother. How do you say no to your mother when she offers you a drink?

-Maggie.

What could she have done?

#4. Little Tommy

I quit school when I was 14 years old. Even when we were walking to school, when I was young, police would stop us. It was only six of us. They would ask us where we was going. We said, "to school, where do you think?" Back then, we didn't sell drugs, we heard about it and all the money you can make and you don't need a job. Just dope and you can make it. So I tried sellingandeveryday "thewhiteman",thepolice would mess with me. Every day, "why are you not in school?", all these questions and they said, "we will call your mother!" I told them she don't care. She's on drugs too. I sale toher. This is what I said to myself. So I got smart, I started hiding until 3:00 everyday, and they don't see me so they couldn't mess with me.

After 3:00, they can't say nothing. I hate police because they always mess with black people. Even though I'm in a drug area don't mean I'm selling drugs or using. We don't have a phone som amacaint'receivenophonecallsfromthem nor school, but she don't care anyway nor do those white people at school. Those white teachers, they don't care. The only ones care for me is "My Dogs". My friends and I, we now sale drugs together in the streets all day and night.

-Little Tommy

Was Tommy wrong or right for feeling the way he felt? Yes or No? What would you have done?

#5. Dee-Dee

When I was growing up I had a lot ofpimples on my face and all on my neck. They called me "Rocky Road Rock-Face". No girls would talk to me. No girls even looked at me. I'm in the 10th grade. I hate school and girls. I fight all the time. I never win but I still fight. In my school if you're not a gang-member you're not cool, nor accepted. They fight everyday. They bulldog others. The Police is at the school everyday. In one year, at our school we had 6shootings. And, they love to carry guns, knives and anything to hurt you with. I try to be around those who are not trouble-makers. I'm tired of being judged because of my skin. I know it don't look good but I'll grow out of it. I think that's what my mom said. We can't afford to go see a doctor. I wish we could. Sometimes I wish I wasn't born. I'm ugly. I am very dark with big bubbles all over my face. I hate myself and so do others. I always feel rejected and alone. Even guys don't hang with me. Man! I wished they liked me! I try to fit-in but they always ignore me as if Iam not even there. Man, If my skin looked better I would feel better!

-Dee-Dee

What do you think Dee-Dee felt? Did Dee-Dee have low self-esteem?

#6. Brendy

Men always looking at my butt. My hair might be short but I know baby-got-backs, yea! In my class, I know this teacher don't like me. I have problems with her everyday. So this is what I do, I'm in high school now, so I just sit there. I never answer her and they laugh. Ilike being the center of attention. I got it going on. She always ask me to leave class. She like pickin' on me. And, I think this guy like me in class, soIsometimesgivehimalittleshow. WhenIleavetheclassroom, Iknowhe'slooking at my butt. So I give him a little exact movement. My teacher ended-up flunking me for the quarter but I don't care. It's only one credit. I will make that up in another class, I hope. My grades are not so good but Idon'tcare. D's and C's are good enough for me. I'm tired of this stupid teacher. I'm not learning nothing in her class. She make me sick. How can I learn in her class and she keep messing with me, fronting me off in front of my boyfriend and friends in the classroom? I'm tired of school and their rules. How can I learn anything? She always asking me what I want to be when I grow-up. I told her, I'm already grown, I'm 16 years old! I tell her, I don't know yet. I don't even know if I am going to finish school nor go to college.

-Brendy

Why is Brendy blaming her teacher for everything?

#7. Dariessa

My dad was a Muslim and he told us all about slavery and what the white man did to the black man. He always said the honorable Elijah Muhammad said this or that. He even wanted me and my sister to wear those old, long dresses and hair scarves to school. My mother asked him was he crazy. She said, "My babies ain't going to school looking like that. They are going to church and that's good enough for me and them". I don't want to be a Muslim. I want to live my life with my friends and besomebody. Everybody use drugs in school. My mother smoke weed and drink but she don't allow us to do that stuff. Her husband is my dad. He's cool. He don't drink nor smoke but he talk crazy about the white man is this and that. And I get tiredofhearing that stuff. I sometimes get good grades in school. My best grades were two B's on my Report Card. I thought that was good out of 6 classes. My dad said I can do better. Mama was very happy. My life is okay but I need more friends. All my friends use drugs. And I got sick of them being high. I gotta' get out of the ghetto if I want to be somebody. This frustrates me.

-Dariessa

Was Dariessa on the right track?
What should she had done?

#8. Monique

My mother put too much on me with my brothers and sisters. My older sister is slow. There's five of us. I'm next to the oldest. My little brothers and little sister, I have to help them dress for school and then, I have to get dressed. Now that's a job! My mother works at night. She gets off work at 8:30 AM and the buses come at 8:15. She only have time to take my older sister to school, a special school. I walk my little brothers and sisters to school 'cause it's on the way. It's a lot of work but I know she needs help. I'm only 15 years old. My mother does the best she can do. I have a lot of respect for my mother. I really loveher. Sometimes when she leaves to go to work, weparty on Saturdays. My friends and I. But I put my brothers and sisters to bed but my older sister never leaves, she parties with us. And my friends understand her condition. I'm not doing too good in school. My mother said I'm growing up to fast and she is sorry for that but she needs my help to take care of us. I don't know who to blame. We are just making it. Next year, I may have to quit school just to work and help my mother.

-Monique

Is quitting school Monique's fault?
What should she do?

#9. Tia Tish – Girls Want Attention

"Look at Tia Tish! She thinks she's all that!" My name is Tia Tish and I hung with my girl at Washington High. We are all juniors and we kick butt if any body get out of line. All the boys look at us. The four of us are the best looking girls in the school. These girls are so jealous of us. We fight all the time. Every day one of us has a problem with somebody. I have been stabbed two times and my girlfriend, Banlisha, once. Now we are looking for a gun. We know it's just a matter of time before one of them bring a gun to school. All of their boyfriends are gang members. But they won't give them guns because they need the guns for themselves to act-a-fool with during and after- school. Don't get me wrong, me and my girls ain't looking for trouble but we don't turn-down no trouble either. We are the best in the school, we get a lot of attention from the boys. The problem is this: we are the fly-est and loudest in our group. When we sit, the attention is always on us. We make sure of that. We go to school just to get attention and dress. I don't care if I pass my class or not. I'm not there for that. I'm there for me, my looks and my shape. I'm the bomb!

-Tia Tish

Is Tia Tish the bomb?
What is her problem?

#10. Mo Mo

The school bus is always late in our 'hood. It takes its time and it be cold outside. I need my dad to start taking me to school. He don't have to be to work until 9 AM. He could take me to school if he wanted. Sometimes I walk. In the summer we walk all the time. Sometimes we take the long way home walking from school because the dope dealers and users are out and they're always fighting. You never know when you might get caught-up in a fight or shoot-out. You name it. It could happen anytime in our 'hood. We went to a school dance and they were shooting there, you can't go nowhere in the 'hood with these fools acting-up. I grew up around all this mess. I can't even have fun around here. The teachers act like theydon't care. They act-a-fool in the class rooms, it's hard to learn sometimes. All these teachers, they don't care. Hell, they got their education. They don't have to care. We are the ones that need to learn what they know. There are so many distractions in my life. Around here, life is short. I'm already 12 years old. I grew up fast around here, seen it all. Well, what you can see in 12 years? I blame my 'hood andteachers.

-Mo Mo

Is Mo Mo angry or happy?
What would you have done if you were Mo Mo?

#11. T. C.

Story about Parents Pressuring the Kid

I can't find a job nowhere, not even washing dishes or waiting tables. I don't want to go to college. I'm tired of school. I did graduate. I never been about that gang thang' because most of the hood' is "gang". I play like I'm with it but I'm not. My mother works and works, that's all she do. Her boyfriend works too. I respect him 'cause he treats us good, me and my two little brothers. He talk to them about gangs and why they shouldn't join them. He told me he never went to college and don't have to. He said you can find a job and move-up in your job and do good there. He said while you're in school or collegeforallthemyearsandallthatmoneyyou couldend-uppayingback, youcouldbeonajob making money. And, I listen to him. He said he make $14.75 an hour at the ship yards and that's good enough for him. He said: "You are born- to-die. You live, work, eat and sleep, have fun and before you know it you're 50-60-70 years old ready to die. So go out boy and get you a job. And, quit trying to be a big shot wearing suits to work and Uncle Tom-ming!" I blame him for me not going to college.

-T. C.

Who is T. C. blaming, and why?
Was T. C. Old enough to make-up his own mind?

#12. Warren – Gangs

My name is Warren. I'm 15 years old. They used to make fun of me and pick on me until I joined the gang. Now I'm loved and the same people that made fun of me don't say much now 'cause I am with my boys. And they know we have guns, knives and drugs. Now all the girls talk to us. We skip school all the time and the teachers don't say much to us about anything. Me and my boys talk to all the girls. I'm only 15 years old and the 16, 17 and 18 year old girls try to talk to me. De De has a car and we park around the corner from school. We have a car load of girls all day everyday while selling drugs, and drinking, and smoking. That's all we do. We don't get high on nothing else, just drinking and smoking, that's it. We don't use the heavy stuff. School has become a drag now. I'm having a little more money and girls like me now. And, no one makes fun of me anymore. I feel good now, better than ever. My father is too busy running the streets and my mother's in jail. So forget about school, I like what I'm doing. I'll bet no one will ever make fun of me again. I feel wanted the first time in my life. If my mother was here she would loveme.

-Warren

What is Warren's real problem: lack of being loved by his parents or wanting to be loved too much?

#13. Danielle – Different People

You might think I'm tripping but I went to a white school on the West Coast in Portland. There's not a lot of blacks down there. Portland is only about 2% black. Sometimes they act like I'm not even there. They are so racist down there on the West Coast. My mother told me: people are people. When we moved from the south, my parents said, "You will not grow upin the south. They are crazy down-south". Okay. Now in my classroom you might have 4 – 5 black students out of 30 in the classrooms. You might not like being the few but you do learn more here in Portland. That's my opinion. The schools are more white and I'm learningmore. It's not a lot of noise in the classes and I feel alone sometimes. The blacks are different in the west but I'm tired of being treated different. I want to be around more blacks. I miss the ghettos, as strange as it my seem. I'm not used to being here and I daydream a lot. There ain't a lot of black boys here in school. I told my mother I want to go back and live with my Aunt Lora. She said, "no". I want to be around my black people. I blame whitepeople.

-Danielle

What should Danielle be focused on?

#14. Shawn – Mother Dying

My older brother used to steal from my mother all the time, her money and anything else he could get his hands on. He was on crack bad, very bad. And when she would put him out. Three days later he would come back. He never worked. My mother was a loving soul, never married but had six kids. I was the youngest. I had one year to graduate and I wanted-to, except for one thing. My mother passed and I was broken. My brother was nowhere to be found. My sisters were married and three lived out-of- town. One was in town and she was on drugs. All of my friends were here in Seattle and I don't want to leave. My older sister wanted me to live with her but I said no. I'll make it. I knew it would be hard to live in mother's house. She was only renting it. The streets was my home for a while: selling drugs and going in-and-out of jail. Why did my mother have to leave me with two drug addicts and a house she was renting? I have no will to go back to school nor work. I feel so alone. If she would not have died I may have finished school and made something out of myself. I Blame Her.

-Shawn

*If Shawn had moved-in with her big sister,
her life may have been different.*

#15. Audee

Everyday I'm around so much violence, so much hate, so much evil. I remember one time I was coming down the block, I saw a friend of mine who dropped-out of school, shoot another friend of mine in the head. And, he just walked- off. They were my age, 16 years old. His life is gone and the shooter's life is gone also. I told my father and he just shook his head and said, "They out there selling drugs and drinking". "The sins of the wicked is death", he said. My father is a Pastor. I know he will be talking about this Sunday at church. I always go to church with my mother and two sisters. My mother prays a lot for us because it's dangerous in the streets. No one has any money in the ghettos. My father tell me to be very, very careful. I live about two miles from school. We alwayswalk, soIseesomuchandbeenthrough so much to be so young. We have been put in a ghetto, we don't have the sense in our lives to make it. You won't make it. I blame the devil for all this mess. As he whispers in the ears of the blind, they begin to seeevil.

-Audee

What does Audee mean? Do we always look for somebody or something to blame.

#16. Jeannie – White Girl

I'm a white girl. I live in the ghetto around a lot of blacks and I hang with black girls. I feel their pain. I see it everyday with my girlfriends. We drink, we smoke, we do everythingtogether, if we don't, we might get in trouble with guys raping girls or wanting their girls to see them fight one another just for the fun of it. I'm 16 years old. This is my 3rd year in High School and it's not a lot of whites. It's about 200 whites but it's about 3,000 blacks in our school. It's always something going on at school. We stay away from the parties because there's too much fighting and shooting at parties. But I don't understand why they hate each other so much. I know why they hate white people. I know why white people hate blacks. I want things to change for whites and blacks. I get called names all the time, all day, everyday. Sometimesmeandmygirlgetintoitandwecall each other names. But we don't stay mad at each other, like the outsiders do with us. Life is hard. And, no, it's not fair all the time for different races but we have to change this problem. And, we can. I blame this on hatred, the lack of money, housing and unfair treatment ofothers.

-Jeannie

Does Jeannie see what needs to be done to love each other as a race?

#17. Venus – Racism in School

I know I have a very low spirit and self-esteem. I'm Venus. I'm here in America and was born here just like everyone else. My parents are still poor. I need help. Blacks and whites don't like me. They are ignorant and vile. They play too much. I'm here to learn in school, not to fight. But I got to fight for myrespect. The smaller you are, the more trouble you'll have. I had to move to another part of theghetto to stop all that fighting. People killing each other too. My gang is just as dangerous as they are. You know I don't do anything to anybody. I'm just different. A different race and nationality. And, people like me are not accepted in the 'hood, the "black" 'hood. Why? People are people. I'm not afraid ofanything.

I'm not afraid to die. I'm 14 years old. I just started High School and I know I'm not going to like it at all. The people can't get along with one another. It's too many gang fights, stabbings and violence. I blame them for fighting all the time, hating each other and other races.

-Venus

Is being Puerto Rican any different from the others who grew up in these places?

#18. Rodisha – Drugs and Fighting

It's a lot of Spanish people in my school man! You can't understand what they are saying. They get on my nerves. They think they bad. They always looking at you like they are better. The girls be getting pregnant at 13 – 14 years old. At my school, Black and Spanish people are always fighting. One black guy shot one of them in the chest for calling him the "n"-word. The gangs don't get along at all. Its a lot of police in our school but people still sell drugs, fight, and shoot dice in the restrooms and in the back of the playground. I'm not feelin' this school. We just moved down here, my mom, dad and 3 brothers from the East Coast. It's just as bad here as it was in D. C., fighting and drugs everywhere. What's going on? Are they trying to get every kid on drugs in the United States or what? It's everywhere. It's more in the schools than on the streets. Don't get me wrong, I tried drugs but I like being in control of my mind. This is my last year. I only made two friends since I've been here. There are so many females and not a lot of males. I mean a lot of girls. The biggest thing or fight here in school is over a boy, all the time. My uncle died in the war and my mother said that's why it's so many women and not enough men. Hate and wars kill.

-Rodisha

What should Rodisha really be concerned about?

#19. Tyrone – Drugs and Gangs

I'm Tyrone. I'm 58 years old. I was in a gang in school. We had drugs and fights. Back then, people were different. More racism was going on then. Now it's blacks killing blacks. Back then, it was whites killing blacks. Education was different. Blacks couldn't get jobs back in the 60's. There were few jobs, so we had to hustle. We don't have a choice. Blacks have made it now today. Look at us. Even though there's still racism, jobs are available. Who's going to take care of you when you get old, if you don't work? The government is not. Your brothers and sisters are not. You have to work now. All my life I blamed people: the white man, friends, drugs, alcohol, anything and everybody but me. It's all on you, your future is in your hands. Your hands are free to work and use. Write, make whatever you choose to do with them. Your mind works now, use it soon. Now you grow old and things work slow. Move on your education while you can. Don't blame no one. Don't blame nothing for your failure. You can be what you will be.

-Tyrone

Tyrone has lived through gangs and many other issues. Is he still living in the past?

#20. Rhoda – Mother Dying of Cancer

My older sister raised me. My mother died, when I was 6 years old. I loved mymother. Cancer was her illness. I cried every night when my aunt and big sister talked about how wonderful she was and didn't know I was listening. My aunt left and my sister raised me. Even though my aunt helped my sister with my mother she never let me forget my mother. She talked about her all the time, looking at her pictures with me. As I grew up, I kept in mind who my mother was, I could only remember very little about her but those memories were good. And then my sister at the age of 36 became sick. She worked hard all the time. My aunt was old by then. I was 26 years old. I just started college because my grades wasn'tso good and I had to do a few years of summer school to graduate from High School, but I did it. My first year of college fell out beneath me. I was torn from my sister's sickness. I knew she wouldn't make it by just looking at her. I had to dropoutofcollegeand gotowork, payrentand live on my own. I don't know how responsible I had to be just to take care of myself. Mymother left me, then my sister left, then my aunt after her husband died. Now who do I blame? God? Is Hereal?

-Rhoda

What will become of Rhoda? Will she give-up?
Will she recover?

#21. Deborah - Talking About Meth

Itookmyfirsthitonmeth'inthebathroomin High School. I was in the 11th grade. This girl had some. She asked me if I wanted to try some. I said, "Yes. Why not?" I been doing it ever since. Meth' is very good. Your high never comes down for days. Meth' is easy to get and you love sex when you're high. I feel good when I smoke meth'. Everybody is doing some kind of drug in my school. Pills, crack, meth', weed, fizz, heroin, you name it, it's there in abundance. I still go to school or class "high". The teachers can't tell. I talk a lot when I'm high. My teachers are so slow when it comes to being able to tell if you're high on drugs. Girls are shooting dope and smoking anything we want to do in the restrooms. They come in andsmell the smoke but they thinks its cigarettes. And, they say, "Girls no smoking in this school. Don't you hear me? You're breaking the rules!" I won't be doing drugs that long, this is just fun- time for a few months. It'll pass and I'll start back into the books soon. If the government would stop drugs from coming into the United States, I wouldn't do them. I blame the government.

-Deborah

Deborah is being silly if she thinks drugs are easy to stop without help.

#22. Steva – Prostitution, Stealing and Cashing Stolen Checks

I'm my witness. I know I've been different and hard to understand. But my looks comes before anything. I used to steal my clothes. My mother could only do so much. I mean, my clothes wasn't from the Goodwill nor second- hand stores. My mother wanted me to look good but when she lost her job and got on welfare, my clothes got scarce and started to look old. So I had to keep my appearance up. So when I started stealing, I was very good. Unstoppable. And then, my luck ran out. I started going to jail learning other trades: cashing checks, selling drugs and prostitution. I chose prostitution. Why? Because it's easier than the other hustles and less time in jail if you were caught. And, I liked it. I liked being out on the streets, in the mix. You know, I stopped going to school. I started full-time prostitution. Traveling to different cities with my man. You don't want to be out there without a man. Protection is very important. When other pimps know you have a man, they won't take your money from you. Maybe I was moving fast but I knew I didn't want to go back to school in them old clothes and I knew my game was good. And, the money I could make was good and enough to get over. My mother blames me but I blame her.

-Steva

Steva wants to look good instead of being educated and learning how to make her future. Where will Steva end-up in life?

#23. Melva

I went to a party after-school. Well, a few hours after-school and that's the first time I tried fizz (ecstasy). My boyfriend said sex is great being high on ecstasy. So, I got high. Everyone at the party was drinking, smoking and having fun. I was so high I forgot what I did with him that night 'cause drinking and ecstasy don't go together too good. I was more drunk than anything else. I had to get home before my mother came home but I passed-out and so did he. I got grounded for 2 weeks and no phone calls, straight home from school for 2 weeks. Mondayatschool, thepartywasthetalkofthe school. A lot of people were there. People was so drunk, they forgot who was there. I know I likeecstasybutIcan'tdealwithnotbein able to sleep. That stuff keep you up. I tried it again a few weeks later. There's a lot of it being sold at school and everybody does it. The girls really love it. I think it's a female drug. Of course men do it too, but females do it more than the males. But I have to stop because you don't get a lot of sleep. You be tired coming to school. Sometimes I just don't care. I love getting high.

-Melva

Is Melva stuck in peer pressure? What do you think?

#24. Tony – Stealing Money

My name is Tony. My father was a hustler and my mother was a "woman of the night". When I was 15 years old, I had my first girl. She was 17 years old. She was beautiful and fine. My father even tried to have my girl. We both dropped out of school to be with each other. My mother and father know The Game and don't even care about my whereabouts. The school would call and they told them I was out of town with my uncle. We were the perfect couple. Every night we did something. Every night we made money. It seemed as if we would last forever. One day after two years in the streets, I needed some guidance for the first time. I asked my father for some advice and what I should do with my money. I hadmore money than I needed and he said, buy some drugs and invest in more money. After I gave my father $2,500 to invest, one month later he was broke. And my money was nowhere to be found. My father and I got into a big fight about my money and how he was to pay me back. I found out he was on drugs and my father ended-up in jail. Mother is on drugs and my girl is in jail for old charges, and new ones. Now I was alone for about one year. I knew I wasn't cut-out for this life. But I was 21 and with no education, college was out. A new decision had to bemade.

-Tony

Was it too late for Tony at the age of 21 years of age?
What should he do?

#25. Steve – Low Self-Esteem

I had thick eyeglasses and bucked teeth. I'm 17 years old. I'm a senior in High School. I play no sports and I am an "A" student. I help a lot of class mates with their homework and different assignments. I'm in church. I don't have a girlfriend and I'm alwaysbeing picked on by girls and boys. My teachers love me and that creates a problem between the envious and jealous ones. I'm also known as "the scientist"or "The Doc'". I'm very smart when it comes to books but I can't understand how to deal with simplestuff:people, communication, girlfriends. Some people say, "Be patient, it'll happen, she'll come and friends will come. Your future is more important than girls right now". But that's easier said than done. I feel picked onfor helping others. I know I'm going to college. My mother and father have good jobs and money put-up for me for college. I love sports but I know I'm too thin for contact. Maybe if I tried to help even more, I'd be accepted. When I go to college I will have some more money to dress better and look better to be accepted by others. I blame the low self-esteem of others.

-Steve

What kind of problem does Steve have?

#26. Brandy - "He's Gay"

I'm gay. I guess you can call me bi-sexual. No, no, I like boys. I was born a boy but I feel like a girl and I know I can't wear what I want to wear at school. So I do it at home. When my mother and father is gone, my little sister help me dress-up. She thinks it's very funny. The guys don't accept me. They say I'm a sissy and make fun of me. It's only a few of us in school but they hide theirs' more than I do. I like to be around the girls but that don't work, they are meaner than the guys towards me. My father don't care for me that much. He knows some thing's wrong. He never take me nowhere, like father and son on weekends. I know he's embarrassed of me. My mother keeps telling me I'm a boy not a girl. She said when I was small I played with dolls too much. She is very disappointed in me but I can't help the way I am. I didn't ask to be like this. My feelings have given me hope. One day, I will be a girl. That's what I am. Why don't they understand? I blame my mother, father, all the girls and boys for not accepting me for who I am and how I feel.

-Brand (a. k. a. Brandy)

What do you think Brand (or Brandy) should do?

#27. La' Toya – She Was Ashamed

Well I'm Marlin the Pee Pot. My sister "pee"s the bed a lot. I used-to also but I don't any more. I never smelled my own self but other girls say I smell like pee. My little sister sleeps with me. We have five in the family (and seven, including mom and dad). I don't have time in the morning to bathe. At night, my mother made us bathe. So now I know why I smelled like pee because the mattress soaked-in thesmell.

Sometimes it would be wet. My mom changed the sheets but the smell was there. I went through hell. I have no boyfriend! Girls didn't want to be around me too much. Even when I tried to smell better as I got older, that smell stayed with me. I don't know but if I just got up a half an hour earlier I could have showered and the smell wouldn't have been on me. If I knew five years ago what I know now, I would have been accepted. I would have had friends and went to parties like the other girls. My life wasn't so good in grade school. I had to figure it out for myself how to get that smell off me. I blame my mother, I needed more help from her, she was too busy working.

-La'Toya

Does La'Toya think too much of herself as she grows up? he's only 12 years old. Does she need a boyfriend or girls that accept her?

#28. Larry – Not a lot of Attention

I had it hard in school. I was slow. I couldn't pick-up on things so fast like the others. I had to go to a special class because of my learning disability. My father used to really get on me about my grades. He told me all the time, "Boy, you're not going to be dumb. You can't go out and play until your grades pick up!" My mother wanted to work with me. She was working all the time and at church on Wednesdays, Fridays and Sundays like clockwork. She never had time for me. She never studied withme.

Church, Church, Church, that's it. My grades was more important than Church and Monday Night Football. My father was glued to the T. V. My little brother got all the attention. I needed help because I don't like being in no special classes. I know I'm normal. I'm not stupid. I'm just like anybody else. I sometimes just don'tget it: math, reading, history. I just need a little help. I'm just as smart as others in other things, like, with my hands I am very good, I can fix things. It's my mother and father's fault, she's too busy in church and he's too busy watching sports. I really needthem.

-Larry

#29. George – Talks About Food All the Time

I'm George. I'm a big, big boy. I weigh 293 lbs. I'm the center on the football team. Nobody can come through me but I have only one problem. I need a girlfriend. I'm good at football but I have no romance and "game" when it comes to talking to girls. I have plenty of game in my favorite sport but girls ain't around me. I'm a sophomore in HighSchool.

I'm 16 years old. I think the Pro.'s might want me but no girls want me, I'm still a virgin. I'm too fat. Even the big-figured girls hate me. My coach loves me. The other guys sometimes talk about me behind my back but they know I am pretty tough. I can also wrestle pretty good. I eat, and eat. Three to four 'burgers, a 32 oz.

Coke, two large fries, that's lunch. My mother tells me I am eating her "out-of-house n' home". It's a joke. My father is a big man but not as big as I am. He comes to my games. He loves sports. He really has a lot of energy when it comes to sports and my games. My mother is very supportive. My mother believed in cooking a lot of food, big dinners 3- 4 times a week. My sister is a big girl too. My mother cooks too much food. All the time money is spent on food, a lot of money. I think if my mother wouldn't cook so much food, I wouldn't befat.

-George

Is George's mother at fault for his size?

#30. Ronnie – The Color of HisSkin

Hi, I'm Ronnie a high-yellow black man. My mother's black and my father's black. I caught hell. "Hey, yellow n----! What's up, pretty boy? White boy!" and all kinds of name calling. I had hazel eyes, sandy brown hair, about 5-feet-7 in height. I wanted to play football, even the team was talking about me. I said, "Say man, I'm black." They would say, "Yeah right! We know yellow-boy!" I had to fight everyday after school, the dark-skinned boys. The girls loved me, the guys hated me. I was the youngest out of three boys but my older brothers were 10 –11 years older than I was. My mother married two times. My life in high school was the worst feeling I ever experienced, grade school wasn't this bad. People were older and most cruelwith words. I had to fight in grade school too but high school was a nightmare. Out of 289 days of school, I fought on 220 of those days, when I wasn't running away from fights. I blame black- on-black crime for all of this and the conditions of the ghettos in America: there are too many poor people stuck in a small area trying to survive.

-Ronnie

Why was Ronnie not accepted?
Is he telling the whole truth about how he felt
about dark-skinned people?

#31. Shanrika - Joining Gangs

I had to join a gang. I had no choice. I told my mother about how the girls in the 'hood would fight me all the time. My sister was two years older than I was and my two brothers had already joined (by force). They told me to get with it, do it. So I did. My name is Shanrika and I got with all the drug selling, prostitution and whatever it took to stay alive. It's very dangerous in my 'hood and you got to have a boyfriend. Just because you're in a gang don't mean you won't get beat-down and raped by your own. So, having a boyfriend is a must. I'm 15 years old at the time. I joined the crew to stay alive. My boyfriend beat me and my brother is still in jail and they were from the same set. Murder was the norm in the'hood.

Eventodayyoudon'thearaboutallthekillingin the 'hood. They can't keep up with the murders. I saw so many people get shot, killed, raped, robbed, cut and bleeding. I've seen it all. And, my mother and father still had to stay in the 'hood because of money. Not enough to get out of the hood. I'm stuck in this life. We hope to live over 17 years of age. 10 – 15% of our hood has not made it to 18 years old. I blame my 'hood for myhate.

-Shanrika

Shanrika is not happy with herself nor others. There are many families in the ghetto: white, black, Spanish and all nationalities. Some make it out, some never come out of the ghetto. Who do you blame or is this just life?

#32. Efforts

We must put-fourth great effort to evolve, to live in the moment and to be right where we should be at that moment working and understanding. This is a gift. The path we have placed ourself on at this time is: having the effort to do so. At this time, what is hidden in this day I should learn? What is the meaning of to-day for my gift to evolve? Today I will put- fourth more effort for my joy and peace and surround myself with the moment. I will surrender to the moment and become flexible that day in the moment, accepting the meaning of that day and looking for the hidden meaning and advantage and live in it. I will remain open to all points-of-view and truth will start to manifest to me the hidden meanings of that moment.

> *And you will find you in that moment. You won't be hiding from yourself. You are that moment and that effort came from you.*

#33. Another Story about School Gangs

My energy level is low and you can feel the negative energy around you all through my school. I wish I was somewhere else and not here at this school. It's too much going on, too much standing-around, cutting-class, smoking cigarettes, weed, fighting, envy and hatin'. Why don't they do something about this? The teachers and staff are afraid of these gangs and drug-dealers. I know they are dangerous, I have seen them in action and what they are capableof doing. I know how they feel because it's in me too but I go around those who feel and think-of something good and positive. They just react off of all their negative feelings andthoughts.

They are so angry at themselves and others. All mouths is what someone has done to them. They react to every little thing that comes out of others' mouths. That's why it's best not to say anything but "Hi" or "Bye" to them. And if you don't say hi or bye soft or the right way, they will ask you, "What do you mean? Do you have an attitude with me? Why you look at me like that?" I blame the staff for being afraid of thesekids.

#34. Ernest – Pressured by Parents

Ernest is my name. I'm a freshman in college. I'm here because of my parents. They wanted me to become a businessman because they own a restaurant and they want to expand. They want me to learn this business but I don't want to go into family business. I wanted to rap. I have a very nice voice, so I'm told. I don't want to be stuck in a state nor city. I want to be free to travel while I'm young. I'm not doing well in my first year, which could be my last year. I'm talking with my dad. I asked him, why do I have to live you and mom's dreams? Why can't I live my own dreams. This is not fair. But I was told, "Just in case that don't work, you have-to-have an education and degree in something to fall-on and work with. You must be prepared forthe future. It comes everyday in people's lives and one day it will come in yours". But I can't blame my parents for wanting me to live their dreams. I might want to be a doctor or mayor, anything but a businessman. I'm not happy with this pressure going into my family'sbusiness.

-Ernest

Does Ernest have the right to defy his parents?
Should he be what they want him to
be or be what he wants to be?

#35. Eddie – A Christian Boy

I'm a Christian in the den of The Devil. This school has just about had it. I gave my life to Christ when I was 7 years old. I have to finish high school and then go full-time to Bible College: 10 years of church, praying and reading the Bible. I still find myself wanting sex and fighting for my respect. These kids are evil and crazy. All they do is fight, gamble and party.

Drugs are even taken in the schools. Killing in the halls of an institution of learning. Gangs running around disrespecting their elders, those who want to help to educate the poor fools who don't have a way to learn. Their futures are in their hands but they think life is a game. An easy way out is hustling and rapping. They are growing into bigger illusions day-by-day. Even if you want to be a rapper you have to be educated to write rap. To be somebody important, you must learn how to share, love, care, trust and hope. These kids don't care about education. Is it the teachers or parents that hold in their hands the future of these kids in schools that have become more dangerous than the streets? I blame this on the Devil.

-Eddie

Is Eddie living an illusion himself or does he have a good point?

#36. Demetria – Mother & Daughter Motivation Story

Demetria is my name and I'm mad I had to move from hell to hell instead of to a better school. This school is no better than the other. I asked my mother, why can't you find a better job? She said because she don't have a college degree and you need this to go somewhere in this world. She said: "I would have gotten a better education when I was young, now I have to work for peanuts and get state assistance to help pay bills and, you all have to have nice school clothes and food. That's why I want you, girl, to go to college and get a degree and be somebody". I said, but mom these kids are worse than the other kids at the otherschool.

There's more students and gangs here. I'm not happy here. She said, "It'll have to do, we can't afford to move anywhere else. You can do it! I know you can. Help me with your two sisters by being strong for them and yourself. Don't make thesamemistakeIdid, youwillregretitoneday as I do today". I said, mom I need to know one thing. If you could do it again what would you have been? She said, "a counselor to help people. And get these kids off drugs, out-of gang violence and motivate the young mind". I said, I will go do what you could have done. I'll help. My mom said, "Thank you, baby".

-Demetria

Demetria is only 15 years old. She's very sharp. She learns fast. Will she make-it?Does she have the right attitude?

#37. Motivation

    6 out of 10 parents or more, don't have a college degree. These parents work in labor, at the shipyards, hotels, motels, restaurants, construction, on assembly lines and do all kinds of labor to support their families. Many households, black, white, Spanish, all groups of people wished they would have finished school and lived their dreams. So many regret their pasts and what they have done with their lives. For a lot of them, their way out was drugs, to numb the pain of failure and justifying their mistakes in life. Church has helped many addicts. And, programs have freed them from drug addiction. Some of these parents that are now in their 50's, 60's and 70's don't have S. S. I. nor retirement coming from a job or the government, no pension nor nothing to survive on financially. This is how they live in the ghettos of America. Their pasts now hurt them, for their own hands have bound them to the chains of poverty. Lost in spirit and in the ghettos in a little apartment or a project in the ghettos, is where they will remain until they die. A life existing, not living up to what they could- have-been and done if they only knew then what they know now.

Will you be like this?

#38. Hakim – A Muslim's Story

My name is Hakim. I'm a Muslim. I don't like the white man's education. We as black people need our own schools to teach what The Most-Honorable Elijah Muhammad taught us:to have our own businesses, land, schools, grow our own food and take care of ourselves. As a black men and women, in this world, we can do it. We don't need the slave master to teach us how to grow food or teach our ownchildren.

We must do for self if we as a nation of people want to survive in this world. There's enough black people to start creating our own living conditions and we will treat each other equally, with respect and dignity, always. If we fight for our freedom, to be free as Americans and if they would give us our own state which they owe us, "40 acres and a mule", then we would create a people of respect and discipline. Men and women who can and will show the world we are righteous people. We are the Original man of this Earth, the first and the last. And, the white man's school just brainwashes our people. I blame the white man for the misuse of the ex- slaves and I blame their education system because they teach nothing.

-Hakim

Hakim is living in the past, is angry and hating in the spirit-and-heart of those who think like him. What do you think?

#39. Salisha – She Killed Her Father & She Likes Women

My father beat my mother all the time. My name is Salisha. I was doing good in school. I'm 16 years old and I love school. I was getting goodgradesandeverybodylikedme, Igotalong with everybody. My father would get drunk everyday and night after work. Never no peace in the house. Fights and fussing all the time. I could move-in with my older brother, he's in another town. I got one year left in school and then I'm going to college. My mother said I'm good at designing things and I was going to go as an Interior decorator doing houses, homes and offices. You name it, I'll be able to makeit come alive. One night my sister and I was inmy room and we heard him beating my mother. She was crying and hollering and I couldn't take it anymore. I went and got a knife and while he wasbeatingmymother, Istabbedhim3timesin the back of his neck. I didn't mean to kill him but to just get him off of my mother. I hated my dad for beating her and so did my little sister. I blame my father for my setback in life. Now, I like women and hate men. I did 15 years in prison.

-Salisha

What would you have done in Salisha's place, hearing this every night? What would you've done if you were Salisha, having to hear this every night?

#40. My name is Melvin

Even in Black History books, white people come to the aid of black people. Even on TV, little black babies in the laps of white people asking people for money to feed them. In my classroom we ask why is it black people can't help themselves if given a chance to. Our savior is White America. People save our little black babies because we can't. I want to know: why do blacks accept this way of life? Just because a few blacks have money and TV shows this doesn't mean that the other 38,000,000 blacks are okay here in America. And, just because we have a black President doesn't mean blacks are notstillbeingkilledintheghettosofAmerica. And in the courtrooms of America blacks are still being set-up and given more time than whites for the same crime. Obama can't stop the killing, the drugs and the pain. Since Obama's been in office blacks are catching more hell.

White groups are now raising more hell all across America, arming themselves for a revolution. They said, "We must take America back!" Back from whom? From Obama? But this is not what they are saying but their actions are. My school has a lot of whites and they show the fear of blacks coming together. They fear unity in the black spirits. They fear the black man loving the black man. They fear the black man helping the black man and the drugs are more available now than ever in the history of America. They say, "Now, if we don't give youajobbutwegiveyoudrugsandalcoholyou will kill yourselves" and thisworks.

Is Melvin living in the 60's? Melvin is 58 years old, he can't see change. Can you?

#41. Andy – Name Calling

I couldn't wait to turn 18 to join the Army. My name is Andy and I'm 16 years old. My mother and father support my future in the Army, so I'm here to finish high school and join the army. Sometimes I daydream in class, imagining myself with my uniform on saluting the officers and holding a rifle in my hand. I'm really looking forward to my adventure. I hope to be a Captain and flying over the world, helping others and keeping the Americans safe from terrorists. I'm not doing good with my grades in school. My father asked me to pick up the pace. My nickname is Four-Eyes. I have red hair and thick eyeglasses. I will have contacts lenses before I go in. I know I'll need them to see better. If I go in with thickglasses they may not let me in. I feel good about my going in. I can ignore the name calling because I know they want trouble. I do have a girlfriend who also wants to join in the Army. She's 15 years old. I hope she still feel the same way in 3 years. I would love to serve with her. I do blame our government for what they have caused in this world. A superpower must play God to control the world. Life is not fair nor are somepeople.

-Andy

If Andy feels this way about the government, then why does he want to go to the Army?

#42. A Buddhist's Story

Hi, I'm a Buddhist monk. We believe in the Krishna consciousness. I had to quit wearing my garment. People made fun of me saying, "Take that dress off! Your pretty orange dress is pretty, sweetheart!" But as they call me names I chant, Hare Krishna, Hare Krishna, Krishna, Krishna, Hare, Hare, Hare Rama, Hare Rama, Rama, Rama, Hare, Hare. This cleanses one's heart of all material dirt. I tried to stay in control of all my thoughts and feelings. I chant all day, everyday to grow spiritually and over come this world's hatred, brainwashing and deceit. I put on street clothing to blend-in and be accepted. I'm a young man. A child of Krishna. It's only about 23 of us here in school. A few of us decided to blend in, the othersdidn't think it was right. So we put our clothes under our garments back-on. A world of confusion just can't accept difference and changes. People are people. Who do we blame for our troubles and problems, heartaches and pain? I blame the demon-gods, the dark forces who control people's weaker selves anddesires.

#43. Jeremiah – Gang Fight

I was in a shoot out with 4 other guys in the 'hood. They ran down on us with guns, in a car. I was hit two times, 2 got killed. Now I'm paralyzed. I have to go to a special school. I was in the wrong place at the wrong time which happens everyday in the ghettos. Someone is always getting shot. My mother said none of this that happened to me was on the news. It happens so much everyday, all day, the news can't or won't cover all the shooting and killing in the ghetto. For life, I'm in a wheelchair never tobeabletorun, walk, playsports, allbecauseI live in the ghetto. I'm 15 years old. My life is over. They say it's not but to me it is. My girlfriend left, my friends never come seeme.

The one's who you thought was with you are not, they are too afraid you are going to ask too much of them. I'm in need and the help I need they can't do no way. My mother and little sister doforme, rightnowI'mstrongenoughtoliftmy own body in and out of the tub (and in the restroom too). But I never thought this would happen to me and there are a lot of "me"'s out there who think like me. I blame black people for not liking each other, they hate each other andiftheydidn'ttheywouldnotkilleachother.

-Jeremiah

Jeremiah thinks it's too late for him. He hates the decision he made. Now he's in a wheelchair for the rest of his life. Let your dominant thoughts prevail and you will appear there! Control your destiny. Whatever you think that's what you'll become.

#44. Dorisha – Girl BeingPicked-On

My mother had to pretend her and my father was not together because we could not afford day care for my little brothers and sister and go on welfare because she couldn't work. So my father had to watch his step because the welfare office would check now-and-then. My father worked on a construction job sometimes 10 –12 hours a day for a little bit of nothing, 7 to 8 dollars an hour. He had a bad back but he still went to work. Mama used to rub his back, neck and the side of his head to relax him from his hard day's work. I was about 13 years old. My mother started baby-sitting just to help daddy out. I don't dress too good because money was tight but they did the best they could dressing me. I'm the oldest out of four, mama anddaddy really love each other, never fight, always hugging and she would kiss him all the time. My problem in school was with this one girl who hated me for no reason. I mean, I didn't dress nice. I had just started liking boys. I was in the 8th grade. She had short hair, so did I. She was dark-skinned, so was I. She had pimples on her face, so did I. I don't know why she and her two friends would want to fightme. The boy she liked, liked me, not her. I blame him now that I think about all of it. I think he wanted to see usfight.

-Dorisha

What do you think of Dorisha?

#45. Tanisha

It seems like every boyfriend I have leaves me after 3 months. I've had 4 boyfriends and about 15 fights. Ex-girlfriends and their friends called me a bad name. "You slut!", they said. "You like sex too much!", they say. Maybe I do but that's my business. I'm the talk of the school, "The Slut". I'm so angry at these rumors. So many boys want to take me to bed, they come right out with it. I told them I'm not like that.

They say, "That's not what we heard". I'm looking for a boy friend not sex. Sex will happen during the relationship. Sometimes I can'tthinkrightfromdaydreamingaboutagood boyfriend. I'm 16 years old. It's time I think about my future. I'm in the 10th grade and I will find a good boyfriend, they can say what they want to about me. I'm not going to college, I'm going to be a mother and have a lot of kids, welfare will help me just like it helped my mother and my brothers and sisters. I want these girls to be so jealous of me! I blame them for giving me a hard time. I'm smarter than them. They want to go to college, I don't, the government will help me. I have it all planned- out.

-Tanisha

What is Tanisha's mistake?
If you could talk to her, what would you tell^nher?

#46. Debra – About Blacks

I'm an "A" plus, 4-point-0 student. I read a lot. My mother and father are very educated and they want the same for me. They push me all the time. They say, "Debra there's plenty of time for boys. Right now focus on education, please. The teacher's are there to teach those who want to learn". I read books at home all the time. I found one book very, very interesting, PostTraumatic Slavery Disorder (P.T.S.D.). I studied this book. It's about black people, what happened to them in slavery and the mental problems slavery caused. Post Traumatic Slavery Disorder. It speaks on the problems blacks have and why they hate one another and the Willie Lynch brainwashing the slave- master's did to the poor slaves. Afterreading this book and studying it. I found the problem of the young youths a wanting to be loved. This is why the spirits of blacks are divided, and why black-on-black violence is so popular. I was so impressed with the author of this book. I wrote him and asked If he could help the blacks at my school. This knowledge is needed. Our black brothers and sisters are lost, they need help, big- time! He never wrote back to me. I will write a book about what I learned about the author's book and what I see everyday. I will learn to help all people come to their truesevles.

-Debra

Is Debra on the right track? If not, how would you put her on the right track?

#47. Derrick

We moved from Los Angeles (L.A.) to "Down- South". I have never seen so many blacks afraid of white people in my life. "Yes Ma'am", "No Sir". I never seen nothing like this it is very shocking to me and my little brother and two sisters. We could not get used to saying, "yes Ma'am", "no, Sir" and we call it "Kissing Butt", "Uncle Tom-ing" and "Bojangle-ing". These are the elderly people. Some of the square, young people down here do the same thing as the elders but the street youth are different from all the others. They are hardcore, they don't play. They are very dangerous more so than the youth in the City of L.A. They are hungry for money and glitter, cars, they like to dress if they have the money. They are really strange inmy school, they live a partying and fun life. Not all of them are like this but a lot of them are. The girls are very different than the ones from L.A. I never seen so manypoor people, even though in L.A. the blacks are homeless and dangerous. But it is so different here in so many ways. I fearformylifedownherebecauseIdon'tknow how they think. In L.A., you can almost tell how people think and where they are coming from.

It's very different here, they are so jealous and envious here. My name is Derrick and I blame those blacks for not standing-up for themselves.

-Derrick

#48. Rita and Sita – Street Violence

I have a twin sister, we do everything together. Sometimes when I want another friend she gets jealous of me and I make excuses to my friends why I don't have time for her. We are 13 years old and in the 8th grade and we look so much alike people can't tell us apart. Mama sometimes mixes us up by names. We live in a very violent 'hood. Right out of our window we can see prostitution, drug-selling and fights. We hear gunshots, police cars racing downthestreets, redandbluelightsallthetime, everyday and night, 24-7, non-stop. I just wonder, who died tonight? Who overdosed tonight? What are they fighting for? Which prostitute died tonight? On our way to school yellow tape is everywhere, police are still on the crimescene.

We talk about our 'hood all day in school, about what might happen next. Never will we do what we see in our 'hood and across the streets in the ghettos of America. There's always some kind of kidnapping, rape, children missing, violence, it never ends. This makes my sister and I closer and love life more, to work hard in the books and study to be the best we can. Regardless of the differences and violence in our school, we must complete our education and get out of the ghetto.

-Rita and Sita

What are your comments regarding Rita and Sita?

#49. Shanisha – Self-Centered Girl

My mother said I put on too much makeup and if I spend half of the time putting on my make up trying to look pretty, I could have a pretty good education. I love to look good, pretty and dress nice. The other girls do too, well some of them. We like attention. I know I'm pretty. I bring out the best look in me all the time. My whole day is centered around how I look. I live in the ladies room putting on makeup and fixing my clothes on me to look perfect, the best I can be. They always looking. I act like they are not even there. I know they are looking at me, I pretend like I don't know they are. I like this football player but he has a girlfriend and she is so ghetto! She acts like a slut, a woman of the streets. Short skirts with high-heel shoes and a lot of makeup. I hate her. She has what I want but they've only been dating for 5 months. I can take him from her, one day I will! When she's not looking I smile all the time at him and he always smiles back. I want to be a model. I look good. I'm smart, tall, and pretty.

My grades are not that good but I'm young! I have plenty of time for school.

-Shanisha

Is Shanisha focusing on the wrong things?
How will her life turn-out if she doesn't study
more and pick her grades up to a good level?

#50. Black Americans

Yes I'm black and I'm an American. Not a Black American, just an American. If you see what I see, hear what I hear, doing what I'm doing you would understand why it makes no difference about your race, nationality or where you're from. I used to think like a lot of you, blaming something or somebody. I knew Icould do anything I wanted after I woke up to me as a human being and not a color. We see ourselves through our own failures or successes. If we know not to fall into the Race Game and live in the human reality of our being, we will start to see truth, love, happiness and prosperity. Why? Because our energy is focused on positive loving and caring for others and self. There will be no room to think of other negativethings because you are so engulfed in love, caring and being the best you can be. My name is Tyler and I'm a manager in a Nike warehouse.

-Tyler

#51. Melvin – A Boy That Likes Boys

Igoonlineallthetimeandtalktopeopleand I know it's wrong to talk to kids on-line under- age. I'm in the 12th grade. I talk with 10 – 12 – 14 year old boys on-line because no girls, nor guys seem to like me. I need a friend. I never talk about sex. I have met a few of them at parks and the boys were 15 years old and they feel the same way I do. We talk about things like: boys and having problems with girls. Do I like boys or men?, that is what I ask in the back of my mind. And, the answer is: Yes, I do like younger boys. Is there something wrong with me? I ask this all the time. I need agirlfriend.

I'm a virgin. I need sex but girls don't like me and the boys I talk-to like me. And, I like them. Am I gay? Does this mean I don't like girls? I like girls. I'm in the 12th grade. I'm 18 years old. I'm not a child molester. I have a little brother, 12, and a little sister, 14 years old. I don't mess with them nor think about it. School don't hold no interest for me. College don't hold no interest for me. I must find myself. And the deep desires I have for boys and young men must subside. I blame my father for not being around. I needed a real man aroundgrowing-up.

-Melvin

Is Melvin okay with girls? What happened in Melvin's life? Is on-line dating okay for young people in their 'teens? Where do you draw the line? And, at what age?

#52. White Americans

We are not animals. We are human beings. My name is Jay. I'm an American. I'm a person who cares and lives fear-free. I know what it takes to live here in America and get what it has to offer. We all have this opportunity to be our own person and choose our future from a very young age. We are so rich in opportunity, education and love for our fellow Americans.

We are a group of people who lead the World in the pursuit of happiness and freedom, reaching- out to other nations. We help and support them, giving them a government they want and need, showing them how they can protect themselves and rule themselves with peace and love with their citizens, as we show here in our great nation, America. My name is Jay. I'm a nurse and I love helping the American people.

-Jay

#53. Ethiopian Americans

I'm Solomon. I was born here in America. My family has been here over 60 years. My father worked all his life running a grocery store. My mother helped him sometimes. As we grew-up, we were taught how to work the store, stock the store, order, keep it clean and provide good customer service. My family and I, we are business-minded people . I'm going into business management. I like business and customer service, people are cool. The American people support each other inbusiness, they buy and sell to each other, giving you opportunity to grow with the American Dream. We as Americans are remarkable people, successful people, people with integrity and leadership ability. We know where weare going and I ride with the working class. I see nothing to blame. Failure is your choice. First look around you, look at other's success, listento their success stories and do what they did and are doing and you can't fail. They didn't, nor willyou.

-Solomon

#54. Nalisha – Missing Little Girl

Mylittle sister was kidnapped at the age of 9 years old. My school was very involved in helping out with flyers and the support was outstanding. I had to stay after school one day and we only live 10 blocks from school and I didn't know she would walk by herself. I asked her to wait. I pray every night and say, "God please bring my little sister back home, please." My mother blames me. I had an incident in class. I'm in the 8th grade. She's only in the 4th grade. She's kind of big for her age. And she knows the streets as far as not to talk to strangers. We worked-hard looking for my sister for days, then weeks. 6 weeks later someone let her go and she was found around the homeless people asleep with this lady. And, the lady said when she woke-up the little girl was there. So many other kids are found dead but she had been raped many times. She was on the other side of town about 15 miles from home. She doesn't remember who the people were. They kept her in a room with a little boy. She said they ate McDonald's food and peanut butter sandwiches everyday and had water to drink. A lady gave them baths and different men would have sex with her. She said it wasn't the same guy. She saw their faces, white, black, and other men. I blame myself for being late after school and not watching my littlesister.

-Nalisha

Little sisters are tough to watch and keep-up with sometimes.
Is Nalisha wrong for how she feels?

#55. Pleasure

Suicides are very common in the ghetto. But you never hear about this on the news the next day. Suicides are big in the black communities. There is a lot of killing I know but they do take their own lives. In our apartment complex 15 people or more in the last 5 years have committed suicide inside of the building. So many people find themselves at the point of suicide whether it be drugs, or shooting, or jumping off a building or out of windows. How they choose, they come to the conclusion that they don't want to live like this here in the streets, the ghettos or their life has no meaning. Even in school, we have had a few of them and I'm not surprised. More people should be looking into the sickness of the suicides that go on in the schools or the ghettos. It's a condition people mentally place themselves in or society drives them to this. They are driven by their own weakness and fears and feelings. They have drove themselves to the point-of-no-return in some cases. My school is just like other schools, if you don't want to be educated and learn they don't care. If you don't care, we will meet you halfway but you have to want to be helped, want to learn and see a future for yourself. We help those who help themselves. I blame it on the institution for not helping these poor people out of the prisons of theirminds.

-Pleasure

True or False?

#56. Doris – Whites Talking About Blacks

We hear about the schools in the ghettos and we laugh at the black people. I know it's wrong, people are people. When white gangs try to come in the schools in the suburbs the police and teachers come together and the problem is resolved quickly. Once in a "blue moon" we have a shooting. I think some of the kids here hear about what goes on in the schools in the ghettos and they start to copy them because they want to be bad or black and tough like the gangs in the ghettos. They want to be like them, but why? Isn't that a "failure mentality"? Not all black people are failures. Our president is black and we have black congressmen and women.

But most blacks are rappers, singers and actors, not doctors and lawyers. There are just a few in the Army as Officers and a few in the world of Leadership. We are the leaders of America. We are the law enforcers and the backbone of America and the world. This is what we went through! And in the ghetto they don't teach this to their students. I blame them, the blacks, for their own shortcomings and weaknesses.

Accept what we give you and work with that.

-Doris

Is Doris right or wrong?
How do you think she really feels?

#57. Martell

My mother is always talking about God. I hate that she speaks on God all the time. God this and God that. Why don't God help the poor, not just black but browns and whites in the schools? But, what about the world? People need help, the little kids on T.V., they needhelp. Where isGod?

God seems to stay out of the ghettos, the deep part of the ghettos, just as the police do. They know the blacks, we kill each other, so they continue to push drugs and bad food in the ghettos, churches and liquor stores right across the street from one another. So before you go to church, have a drink and after church have a drink, go get high. Drugs and alcohol are cheap and easy to get. It's plenty there for your school too, all around the schools this is a way-out-of education. Just get high, you don't have to learn, go to school just to get high. You don't need an education to get high. Go snatch a purse and bring the money to me. Numb your feelings and pain because of your failures, your living conditions and your hatred for self. Come get high and for a while you won't feel a thing. I blame God for allowing the white man to be so cruel and I blame blacks for being so brainwashed.

-Martell

Is Martell feeling good?...even about himself?
Aren't we responsible for our own self?
As we grow we put-aside good and bad
thoughts but we must love humanity.

#58. Larry

I go to a private school. In our school we never had a shooting or a stabbing but weed and meth' is on the rise in our school but we never hear much about these students once the teacher or staff finds out who they are. They are put out and put in drug programs and given one chance only and that's it. They don't play here! If your grades go under a B+, they will meet with you and your parents, and ask, "why?" "Is there something going on at home? Are there drugs? Your family is being investigated". They have counseling for you and your parents, they are very serious about education and leadership, the best you can do and the best you can be! Police don't come in this school and take students out of classes in handcuffs. We don't pull fire alarms in our school unless it is a real fire. Kids don't smoke in the restrooms, nor skip school, then again, well... you might get one or two a year. Most juniors have their own cars or parents pick-up students from school or the parents bring them to school. Teachers are very strict in disciplining students. The teachers don't live in fear in the classrooms. Parents are involved in the school activities with their kids. We are told, "We are leaders of thisworld".

Losers don't come here and don't stay here. If it's money people need to educate their kids, then parents should work harder.

-Larry

What do you think about Larry's feelings?

#59.

What is the difference between black schools and white schools and the education there?

Can't people learn through all of their differences? Do teachers care the same? Is there such a thing as good teachers and bad teachers who are sent to the schools in the ghettos or is it just a coincidence? Does the system send different teachers to the poor partof town and ghettos to purposely not give the ghetto children the proper education? If this is so, then why are black leaders allowing this to happen? What are the differences between the schools and their education systems and how does this work better for whites and not for people of color? It's all about money. There's a lotofpeopleofcolorwithmoneybuthereare 39 million blacks in America. Maybe 4 to 6 million blacks have money to give theirchildren a good education. What about the other 85 to 90% of the black parents in America who are just-getting-by and can't afford private schools of higher learning for their children? People don't think education should be equal, you have the "haves" and "have-nots". Is the world fair or unfair? This is what causes the ghettos in America to be ghettos: people who can't afford to live anywhere else but on welfare and jobs that only pay minimum-wage or a little more money than minimum-wage. Who do we blame for this? Do we blame ourselves or the American government for not giving the black men and women equalrights?

Why live in the past? Live now, in-the-now.
Teach yourself how to be a success.

#60. Sharon – About Black People

We study Black History all the time and this is mostly a white school. A few blacks and brown-skinned males and female go to our school. What I don't understand is why they killed these black leaders and all they wanted was to be heard and help their people out of their situation. We read between the lines. For the most part they were not violent. We were violent towards them. We look at America and see it is changing. I agree but... The blacks who are doing good say, "Yes, America has changed." The ones who are doing bad, they say, "America has only changed a little." But the one's who are not doing good at all, who are doingvery, verybadintheghettossay,"No, no, no! They only want you to think that thingsare changing by giving a few blacks TV shows and rap time on TV to trick you!" What about the blacks who are stuck in the ghettos and want to get out and can't get out? There's millions of them. Over 28 – 30 million in the ghettos and half of them or more are good people and they are really, truly trying their best with what they've got. I know. I live this everyday. I was blessed, my parents were those whites who had parents who wanted out and made it. I'm a white girl, my name is Sharon and I like black people. They are good souls, spiritual people, the backbone of America. I blame white people. They haven't changed much, only enough to keep trickingblacks.

-Sharon

Why does Sharon feel like she feels? Ask yourself this question, "How much has America changed"?

#61. "Success"

If life is what you make it, why do people make it so hard for themselves. I watched my family and other families destroy themselves for the love of money. We can't live without the dollar. People will do many things for money. Sell drugs, steal, rob, sell themselves, lie to you, cheat you and hate you. Will I become like them? Will I steal for money? Will I take responsibility for my own life? Or, will I blame you for my failure? I will fail if I do drugs. I will fail if I join gangs. I will fail if I steal and sell drugs. I have already failed if I don't get an education, if I don't work and be honest andlove my life as I study hard to be somebody, to want more than "the failures". I must love more than failures, care more than failures and knowhow not to fail. I must be all I can be, then I have no one to blame but me for who I am. I will not blame my mother, father, sister, brother, cousin, grandma, grandfather, friends, schools, people, places nor things. Why? It is because the only way to fail is to see yourself failing and not do anything about it. My name is Success. I have high self-esteem, self-confidence and self- control. I love myself, I do to others as I want done unto me. And my friend's name is Positive Thinking. We talk all day everyday and I love my positive and successful life and it's without blame. And, my friends, he and she being twins, they are named Responsibility and Accountability. They make sure as you grow and mature with them, you become self- sufficient, healthy and happy with what you have given that was good and positive in life, and to others in your community and yoursisters and brothers abroad. And this will happen only if your keep your three best friends with you, always in mind. Stay conscious, focused, healthy and active, as you come closer to your goals and you will achieve your heart's desires. Walkit, talkit, beit, liveitandyouwillbecome it.

-Success

#62. Steve – About Blacks

Our teacher told us, "The Black Panthers were not good people. They wanted to take over our government. They deserved to die and be put in jail." I don't agree with her. The Black Panthers wanted to protect the ghettos from the drugs and The police brutality on black people. Yes, some of them hated white people but no more than white people hated blacks. The Panthers wanted to make a difference in the 'hood. In neighborhoods across America, they made them look bad and violent. They lied on the Black Panthers just like they lied on Malcolm X, Marcus Garvey and Martin Luther King Jr. because they were a big threat to the white man controlling the blacks in the'hood.

They had to get rid of those who thought independently and those who stirred-up the minds of black people. The whites don't want the black nor colored people to awaken. Obama is in the house, the White House, because the house is very dirty. And, blacks always clean-up white peoples houses when it is dirty and the White House is no different from the slave masters' houses we used-to clean. Obama is a wise and intelligent man and they know that "white" America hates Obama. Blacks and peopleofcolorknowthathe'llclean-upAmerica the best he can and then they will dirty the house again. I'm not saying Obama is a butler andMichelle'samaidbuttheyareverybeautiful together and their children are as well. I blame American racism.

-Steve

Johnny Richey

Steve sounds angry and mad at Americans.
Should people forget their past and look to the future?
The slaves were treated bad but learn from that and move-on with your education and lives.

#65. Darlene & Mr. Strickland: An Eating Disorder Story

I know my teacher like me. He always asking me to stay after school as if I have done something wrong to fool the others in the class. He look old. I'm too young for him. He's trying to get me over his house all the time. I told my girlfriend. She said, "He's ugly and too old for you". I might be a little on the chubby side and boys sometimes laugh at me. And girls too. But I don't care. Mr. Strickland gives me all the attentionIneedbutIwantthisboy, John, tolike me but he don't. I think I'm going to go to Mr. Strickland's house. I know he want to have sex with me. One time I had sex with my uncle and I was raped. So I know how it feel...but man!

This old man? But I need to be wanted. Mr. Strickland tell me everybody need to be wanted and fit-in with a group of people. Their peers. Those who feel alike and think alike. I'm only 15 years old. I need a boyfriend. All the other girls have boyfriends. Why can't I have a boyfriend? Once, this girl told me that if I want to lose weight, just start throwing-up after I ate and the weight will drop. I might start doing that. I want to look pretty like the other girls.

-Darlene

Should she be having sex at 15 years old?
What does Mr. Strickland want from Darlene?
Are there other ways to lose weight?

#66. Teesha – Being Poor

Hungry is our family's last name. We are on food stamps and we go down in this long line on Saturdays to get a box or a sack of food. We are so poor. I hear about parents using drugs. My parents don't use drugs but we never have food. My clothes are from the Goodwill and my birthday is never celebrated with friends. One time about 10 years ago when I was five, my mother gave me a little cake. But, that was before my other brothers and sisters were born. I'm 15 years-old. My parents have 6 children that's why we are poor. My father works and my mother stays at home with the kids. I work after school sometimes. It's hard for them, I'm worried. My mother worries a lot, I can tell. I told her it will be alright. I'm doing good in school, I will get my family out of the ghetto. My father has a bad back and he's older. Most of the people my age have parents' that are like 39 to 47. My mother is 34 and my Dad is 59 yearsold, hewasanalcoholicforyearsandnow he's clean. He hasn't worked in his whole life but 6 years, no retirement funds but he is doing the best he can do. I love my family so much and I'm going to do everything I can to help. "Food is so high now", my mother said. I blame the recession.

-Teesha

Is Teesha too young to take on so much in her young life?
What would you do if you were her?

#67. Bobby – White School

The biggest thing that goes on in the schools in the suburban areas in mostly white schools is partying and car accidents from drinking too much. It's not as much drugs in our schools as the black schools nor violence, there's a few fights but other than that it's pretty mellow. The teachers are cool and fun too. We only have about 700 students and most of the people know each other and grew-up, somewhat, around each other. We live in a small community, it's only about 125,000 people in our little town. A few of the teachers know our parents. It's only about five black families in our community and we share with them just as we do with whites.

Some of the people don't want them around, you know, the "Old-School" people, 70, 80 and 90 them, "Change with the world. Stop living in the 20's and 30's!" They don't understand. In the last 10 years we have buried about 35 friends and went to see over one-hundred in the hospitals. It's sad even though I was young, about 7 years-old, but I remember putting flowers down on the places where the accidents were. I blame all the alcohol advertising on TV and people who buy under-age kids drinks from the stores.

-Bobby

Is Bobby blaming the right people or should he blame the parents for not talking to their children about drugs and alcohol? What are your feelings?

#68. Demo – Positive Thinking

Our school is rated high in academic performance and graduation percentages. I'm an Alpha' and will be one for life. Now to clarify things, all black schools are not dangerous. We have a few where blacks and all colors can go and learn, even in the ghettos of America. I'm happy to say I go to one of those fine schools in the ghetto. This is my last year in school. I'm going to college and then Law School. I'll be in school for another 8 years after doing 12years.

I will take 6 months-off and start school in January after I graduate in June. I'm ready to complete my goal which is an Attorney-at-Law to help those who need me. I'm happy to say my future looks more than bright. It's where I'llbe. I know fate is in our reach to control our destiny.

The lack of discipline is the weakness of all people who have goals to reach and give-up because the white man, the black man, the Spanish people, whatever your excuse may beis not important. You are more important than the people you think can stop you. We are our worst enemy, not other men or women. I blame the people who blame others. There is a way out of the ghettos, it's called determination, work, discipline, and you will accomplish what youwill.

-Demo

Does Demo have a good point or is he one of the lucky ones? Do you feel lucky like Demo or are you done (finished) blaming others for your own failures?

#69. Ishira – Going to a Drug Program with her Mother

I went to a drug meeting after school withmy mother. She told me they asked her to bring some support to this meeting and I wanted to go with her. I really want my mother clean and sober. I want this so bad and anything I can do to help her, I will. My father left 8 yearsago.

He don't call nor come by. My grandmother buys my school clothes and gives me money, if she has it when I need it. My grandmother is strong and we live with her. My grandfather died 4 years ago. Church was his life, my grandmother still go sometimes. I go with her. My life would be messed-up if it were not for my grandmother. My mother was fired from her job, as hard as it is to get a job with a dirty U.A. (Urine Analysis). Now my mother and I stay at my grandmother's house and she loves that she was lonely. I like staying there, people respect my granny and so do I. After 6 months in this program, my mother looks sogood and she gives thanks to her Higher Self. All the time my grandmother says, "I'm so proud of you"! I'm proud of her too. I said, She's in church now looking good, men looking at her! My grandmother wants her to find a husband 'cause there are good men in church. I blame the drug dealers for selling drugs to my mother and I blame her too for buying. I'm 15 years old, I want to besomebody.

-Ishira

Why does Ishira blame the drug dealers and her mom? Who's fault is it really?

#70. Lilly – The Story Is About a Drug Baby

I was born a crack baby. My name is Lilly. I'm not like others. I'm different because I can't handle stress. I have big issues with stress. I'm on medication. Sometimes I find myself being depressed for no reason, maybe I don't belong here at this school. My grades are not that bad. I do get D's and C's on my report card. My mother told me I'm "special" because I'm good at remembering names of people, animals, anything with a name I'm good at remembering. I help my mother with my two sisters. They are much younger than I am. My mother said she was so sorry for using when she was pregnant with me. I tell her all the time, It's okay, I love you. She said, "Don't feel bad if people tease you or laugh-at you". I told her I'll just laugh back at them and I do. It's so funny when people try to be mean to you. Mama said, just pay no attention to them. Sometimes when I'm catching the bus, this boy says, "Hey baby, where are you going?" I say, to school. And they laugh and I laugh with them. They say I'm pretty. Mama said, "That boy only wants one thing and that's it." I told my mother I would never do that with them. I don't blame my mother, she made a mistake.

-Lilly

#71. Darrin – Track and Field

I'm the fastest in my school. I love Track and Field. One day I will win the gold medal. My gym teacher told me to keep my grades up. I try so hard but sometimes I just don't get it. Other kids learn fast. My gym teacher helped me get a tutor and the tutor is very nice. His name is Mr. Johnson. Mr. Johnson said, I have to learn to put the same effort toward learning as I do running. I asked him, How do I do that 'cause if I could do that, I would be the fastest learner in school also. So he got me one of those little tapesandIgoovermylessons3and4timeslike Mr. Johnson asked me to. Now I'm doing good in school. Sometimes I get a B-, the best grade I ever had was a B. My father said that was so good. He said, "Learn and stay in school. One day you will see what I mean." I'm in the 10th grade and no one can beat me running. My coach said I was "a natural". I was born to run. Last year no school could even come close to keeping-up with me, not even the 11th and 12th graders. I'm so fast! I love being fast. I wish my mother was here to see me. It's been 15 years since she died of an overdose. I was 10 when she died. I cried all the time. My girlfriend said her mother died of an overdose too. On my mother's birthday, I go and visit her at the burial site. Sometimes, I blame my father for not looking-out forher.

-Darrin

Should Darrin blame his father or should he blame his mother? What about the people who sold her the drugs?

#72. "My name is Ebony" - Homeless

I was homeless going to school but they didn't know I was homeless, I never told anyone, I was so embarrassed. I'm 12 years old. My mother said, "Just go in the restroom at the Service Station and wash-up and brush your teeth and go on ahead to school." Buildings that are not being used, we sleep in them all the time. It's so cold in the winter but sometimes the city gives us big thick blankets and it helps. In the snow, the city comes and puts people in rooms, that helps sometimes. I wish we had an apartment like others in school. Sometimes people look at me and say that I stink but I don't smell like they say I do. My teacher helps me with food sometimes. She knows I'm homeless and she will not tell anyone. My mother has no family here. We moved here 4 years ago and I remembered living with my grandmother, it was warm in her house, always food and hot water and I loved to play with her cat. She so cute.

We are waiting for housing, Mama said, and it won't be long. 20 months of this is enough. My mother tells me she's sorry every night and we keep each other warm at night. My mother said it's her fault.

-Ebony

#73. Oscar

I'm in an academy school, a great school. My parents are officers in the Navy. My brother and I will be Officers sooner or later, years from now. We grow in this school, we will be cut off from your ordinary schools of learning. I know things we know are not taught in other schools and it's no fun here. We can't do some of the things the outsiders can do. We can't have the fun others can have. We don't have a choice but when I'm older I can say I'm not going into the Navy. I'm now 16 years old, my brother is 15 years old, we belong to the American government. My brother and I never had the chance to party or smoke weed. We were too closely watched by our parents. We watch the news, we see how we don't want to be. When we go out, we go out in groups of 8. Our parents are at sea and we are watched by our relatives, if our parents are not home. School is not fun to us. We are the future Captains, Majors, and Generals. We are the future leadership of the State. Our parents are very important people and so will we be. My brother and I like the private life. I'm used to it. We don't know any other way. I blame my parents for my fate and so does mybrother.

-Oscar

Do you believe everyone has a choice in what they should be or become in time? Or are some people forced to be who they are?

#74. Lewis

My grandfather who fought in the war and myfatherbothtoldmehowtheyweretreatedby the white platoons and their treatment was worse than how you would treat a dog. There were platoons for whites and platoons for blacks. I was so sad listening to these stories. I hated the way they were treated and seeing is believing. The way they treated blacks in the ghettosofAmerica, rightthereinmycitywhereI live and grow-up, they kill blackseveryday.

And blacks fought to save America just as whites did fight for our country but in our country we are treated like dogs. I couldn't help but reflect back on what my grandfather and father told me. I started hating white people and the streets of the ghetto because this is also war on the black man here in the American streets. It almost seems like no black people ever done anything right nor good here in America. You never hear about nothing good about blacks, not even in school. No war ever was fought with blacks in them, this is what one would think if they didn't know any better. In my school in the classrooms they show blacks as slaves and running-around in Africa naked, with spears, no education and no sense. I blame white peoples' racist hate towardsblacks.

Lewis was in school in the 60's but many things have changed since Lewis was in school or have they? And if so, what has changed? What do you think?

#75. Donna – A Girl Acting Like a Boy

I was born a little girl. I always wished I was a boy. I always did "boy" things, I hung with the boys; I even liked girls just like they did. My mother used to always want me to wear dresses and when I was old enough, I stopped wearing them. I loved looking like a boy. Basketball was my favorite sport we played at the time. I was pretty good, so I was told. I was an only-child. My father just loved me and thought I was his little angel. As I grew up I knew I wanted to be a police woman and Iknew I could do just what I put my mind to. We wasn't poor. My parents worked-hard, whatever I needed they got for me. When I was in high school, my second year, I started rebelling. My mother started telling me, "Look, you were born a girl. You need to act like a girl not a boy." I moved-out at the age of 16 ½. My girlfriend and I was young and silly, not knowing how rough and dangerous it isout-there-on-your-own at a young age as we were. No one would hire us for jobs. No one cared about the predicament we were in. My father, after he found-out I liked women, was very disappointed in me. I went back home and quit school my last year. I want life the way I wanted it. No one could tell me I wasn't a boy. I look like one and feel like onetoo.

-Donna, a.k.a. Don

Was Donna wrong to be what and who she wanted to be?
Did she fight hard-enough for her future?

#76. Doris Monique

I'm half black and half white. Blacks don't like me. Whites don't like me. They call me high yellow or red. My name is Doris not red, little yellow nor high yellow. I get sick of the name calling. There are four or five white people in my school and they catch hell all day everyday. If you're white or light-skinned you catch hell. My mother is white, my daddy is black. And I tell them all the time to shut-up. I'm black, they say, "No you ain't you little half- breed!" I'm 13 years old. I went through this from the time we moved to this sorry town. I am tired. 5 years of this is enough. So I started skipping school in the 8th grade all the time just so I don't have to be around them fools. I flunked a grade when I was in the 2nd grade. I should be in the 9th grade. I'm 15 years old and still in the 8th grade. That's why I smoke weed, good weed, to forget about that mess and what I'm going through with this school. I'm quitting school and I know this. The girls are mad at me. I can't help it if the boys like me. The boys are always messing with me. Damn, only if I could go to another school! Mama says its too much trouble. I'll make it. I'll get a job dancing until I turn 16, then I can work somewhere. My girlfriend said she knows this older guy who pays for sex. I don't know about all that. I mean, I had sex before but not for money. I have to think about that. If I could only try anotherschooltheymightnotteasemesomuch. I blame this on those jealous girls and those haters because I'm pretty and they arenot.

I BLAMED YOU, YOU AND YOU

-Doris Monique

Doris Monique is in pain and young
What should she be focused on?

#77. Tammy

Myuncletoldmeif Isaidanythingabouthim and I having sex, he would tell my mother I'm smoking weed and drinking. He moved in with my mother and sister about a year ago. He got a divorce from his wife. I smoked weed and was drinking before he came. One day he was coming home from work and he saw me and four others in the wash room in the basement of our apartment. And he smoked and drank with us for a while and went upstairs. That's when it all started. He would tell me things while I was high, to scare me and make me nervous. So I couldsaynothingtomamabecauseIdidn'twant her to know I was using. I'll be glad when my uncle moves out. He wants to have sex too much. I told my girlfriend and she toldher brother. And his brother like me but I don't like him. But it's good she told him 'cause he told his mother and she looked into this and my mother put him out 'cause she questioned me and I said: Yes we are having sex. She asked, "How long"? I told her: four months. She don't want her brother going to jail, so she asked him to leave and hedid.

-Tammy

Do you think holding a secret is good or bad?
What secret did Tammy hold?

#78. Joy

My mother made me have sex with men for crack when I was 13 years old. I hated my mother for that. I hate her now. I like sex and can't get enough. I have sex all the time with my boyfriend and other men. I cheat all the time on him. And the other boys tell him I'm cheating but I lie all the time to him. I want to be good to him, but I can't. He's not enough for me. My brother's friend comes over all the time just to see me and have sex with me while he's in the room with his girlfriend. My mother's always out hustling. My father left years ago. I'm on birth control so I can't get pregnant. I have had 4 diseases in 6 months and they blame that on me. I told 6 guys they gave it to me, that's how my boyfriend found out I was cheating. A year later I found out I had AIDS/HIV and my life is messed-up now. They help me a lot with my illness. The clinic is nice and very helpful to my condition. My boyfriend left. Now I have no one but the clinic and the others who have AIDS

HIV too. We talk all the time. My mother don't come see me. My brother does every-now- and-then. I blame my mother.

-Joy

Should Joy blame her mother?

#79. Dontae

My school went on a field trip. On our way, we saw the homeless and how they lived in the streets. A little homeless community of its own people using drugs on the streets, looking in the garbage. It smelled so bad and looked so bad. People pushing shopping carts with bottles, cans, clothes and beddings. On the bus we could smell the odor all around us and the people looked so sad. Police made a lot of arrests in the homeless community becausethey steal a lot, fight a lot and use a lot of drugs. My teachers said some of these people gave-up, some have mental problems, some quit school, some were lawyers, doctors and smart businessmen and women, and gave-up on life and themselves. We were blocks from thembut we could still see the crowd of people around the line. We got there, they were feeding them. It's garbage everywhere, sleeping bags, carts, strange people, most of whom had given-up on life and themselves. And some just had "bad luck". Whatever the case may be, in their lives they need more help than they are given. I blame the government for giving-up on the American people when we need thegovernment most.

-Dontae, age 17

Was this a good field trip? Should more teachers involve students in more of these activities? If students could see more of these kinds of conditions, do you think it would help young Americans to not give-up on themselves?

#80. Hi, I'm Murray

Hi my name is Murray and I hate being African-American. I hate being black. Blacks are hated by so many nationalities. We have suffered so much. I'm embarrassed being black. My father told me there's a spiritual war going on in the streets of America. It looks physical but its spiritual, physical bodies are being used to cover the truth. The truth is being colored by race. The real war is with yourself like all wars that are fought. Self is the leader of hate, racism, rape, murder, envy, you name it, the name is self. If we judge those around us and say, they do this and he did that, she is a drug- dealer, a prostitute, we are the same, we are just like them whom we judge. My father said, "They won't teach you this in school. You must what is right and wrong; what's good for you and others; learn to talk to and treat others like you want to be treated and talk kind to others 'cause you want others to talk kind to you. Be good to yourself and be at peace with yourself and you will draw that which you think and feel". This is what my father told me after I shared my feelings with him. I kept these feelings inside of me since I was 13 years old.

I'm 18. I'm older now. I'm enrolled in school. My father is so happy I'm going to college. He told me we are not colors of human beings. We are spirits in a body experiencing the physical world, we are old souls and we must know why we are here.

-Murray

Why is Murray so angry at life and himself?

#81. Jada

This is the talk around school. That's crazy!

My story is being told from jail. I'm 15 years old. They wouldn't stop messing with me, you know, the boys, making fun of me, feeling on my butt in the halls. Okay? I got tired of that mess. One morning when I got up I was walking to school. My girlfriend and me. I said to her, Larry think I'm playing with him, he always showing-out in front of his friends, talking about me, calling me names and feeling on me. I got something for him today. Let something happen today! Well it happened after lunch. We were in the halls by my locker, my girlfriend and I and here he comes, him and his boys, trippin' with me. He walked up on me and said, "Come on baby, you know you like it". I said, I don't like it nor you, leave me alone and he wouldn't. I took my knife out of my backpack and he didn't see because he was feeling on me. Him and his boys were laughing. My girl kept saying, "Y'all leave her alone", they thought it was funny. I stabbed him 3 times in the chest and he went down. I said, now laugh punk!

-Jada

If Jada would've went and told her parents and teachers what was going on, then this wouldn't have happened.

#82. Solisha – About Having a Boyfriend

My mother told me to go to the Boys and Girls Club afterschool until she came home from work or go to her friend's house. I chose the Boys and Girls Club. I'm 11 years old, my brother is 14 years old and my mother only asked him to keep an eye out for me. But, he don't have to hang with me, I'm his little sister. His friends tease him at times when he walksme to the club. My mom said I'm big for my age and boys don't know how old I am. I look like I'm 15 to 16 years old, she said. A lot of boys tried to talk to me but I'm very shy and, besides, my big brother don't like them even speaking to me. One of the guys who works at The Club is about 19 or 20 years old, looks out for me, my mom made sure of that. My girlfriend and I are very close, we tell each other everything, we talk about boys sometimes but I'm so afraid of them even looking at me too long. Sometimes I see other girls my age talking to boys but mama call them, "fast, hot little girls". Me and my friend have a lot to talk about besides boys, like girl- talk and playing-together. One day I know I'll be older and when I'm in high school I'll have a boyfriend. Right now, "I'm too young", mama said.

-Solisha

Is Solisha too young for a boyfriend?
What do you think?

#83. Steve

My mother said, "school teachers and people are so different. Things have changed". One thing that has changed for sure is what blacks can be today. Back in the old days, blacks were limited, now they can be what they want to be. Times have really changed. When we were coming-up in the 50's and 60's, we couldn't get loans, grants nor scholarships for higher learning from the Government. Our parents had to help and if they couldn't help, then we just graduated from high school and worked a job from there. Mostly labor jobs but it was a job and it paid the bills. Blacks have made it now. If they want to learn, they can. You have to want it so bad to make-it and you will. I know I wanted to be a nurse, so bad, and look atme, son. You can do it too. Your grandma and granddaddy helped me as much as they could. I worked at night and went to school in the day, it was very hard but I did it. And, so can you if you never give-up. I tell all my friends, my sisters and brothers who want to be somebody: If I can do it , so can you." These are the words of my mother. I'm Steve and I blame people who blameothers.

-Steve

#84. My name is Raymond

We are living in a time of wars, drugs, killing and rapes, you name it. It's going on in the streets, people's homes, only the strong will make-it out here in this world. You have to look around you and see what's going on and once you learn as a teenager, if you make it, that you should not be like those other teenagers wholive to kill, sell drugs and not go to school, instead, you should educate your self. Higher learning is the norm, the key to strong survival out in this world. Excuses are not accepted. Dropping out of school is not accepted. Being ugly is not accepted. Being poor is not accepted. Not having a mother or father is no excuse, just because they were on drugs. Once you over come that event, once you get past that stagein life, you have moved-on and let go. And, "do for self" at one point in your life. Whether you be 13, 14, 15, 16, 17, 18, 19 or 20 years of age, when all is lost you can find your self. In all of this world's hatred and unfairness and mother's faults and daddy's abandoning(s), you can rise above this world's differences and cruelness.

My name is Raymond and I change with the times and listen to the teachers in school. And, they will help you learn if you are willing to listen. I blame you for making excuses for your own failures.

-Raymond

#85. Sandra

My teacher said, greatness is in everyone. Greatness is right in front of you, it's your gift. Everyone has a gift, something they can do better than anyone else. Dharma is what it's called. She said we all have a purpose in life, a unique talent and we must find this in ourselves. We must not be selfish. We must serve humanity and our country. We must serve each other to the fullest and give our best to each other and to ourselves. In expressing our love for life and humanity, we become caregivers of those who lack love and hope. People need each other as a baby needs milk to grow. You must grow from hatred and selfishness and fulfillyour destiny and your purpose in life. We must manifest a spirit of beauty, expressingthat beauty so others can see you and reflect what they see from you. What is my purpose? How can I find myself in all of this madness. The whole world is moving around me but I am one. One part of the whole. How can I help? We must first become conscious of our own being, the beautiful spirit that we are and give to those who are also seeking and then, and only then, will we find our true selves and purpose in life. My name is Sandra and I blame no one but me for not helping.

-Sandra

Is Sandra on the right track? Is Sandra someone you would like to be like?

#86. The Story of Success: Purpose in Life

We are here as physical beings manifested to fulfill a purpose. Inside of us all is a divine being (spirit) with a talent and purpose to better this world. We must experience a higher learning of our true selves, we must discoverour spirits that's deep inside and ask, "Why am I here? Who am I here to help besidesmyself"?

When we are aware of our spirit and work closely with other people, we become at peacein a world of chaos. Connecting in the higher realm of our spirits, we learn love and peace as we grow into our unique talent and purpose in life. Loving to give something everyday: hope, caring, peace, love and compassion, we all need this in this world. Today we are living in atime where people are suffering and calling-out for help. And, the response is: "No. I can't help because I need help." People are dying, crying because jobs lost, bills are not paid and have no medical insurance. We must help them, see them and give a word of hope, show compassion, love, and leave them in peace.

Only the strong survive but the strong must help the weak.

#87. Larry

Southern blacks are different from East and West Coast blacks. We moved from the west, to the east and then, down-south. I see the difference in how blacks live, learn and respect one another. Blacks down-south are more friendly, the "square" ones, that is. The churches are different down here too. In my school the kids seem to want to learn and be somebody down here. This is so different from where I'm from. My father sells insurance and the money was better down here, so we moved. I asked my mother if I could stay with my aunt in the west but she said, they didn't have room for me. And, my little brother needed me and she did too. My mother is so sweet and she loves my father. I also got in troublein California and I was shot in the leg and that's another reason my mother wants me home with her. But I have changed, I learned my lesson about gangs and "street life". The teachers down here teach different and the students who really want to learn pay very close attention to them. But, your clowns in the class room are in a different class like for "special" people, hard- to-learn people or students. I'm happy to experience more people's behaviors andfamilies' differences.

-Larry

#88. Native Americans

I'm Little Wolf. Yes I have a lot of hatred in my heart for things that happened in the past. Every group of people has a past. What makes America so great is all the pasts of the many nationalities here in America living together, fighting together, working together, learning together to keep this nation strong and prosperous. We are America, who are the laws of the fundamentals of this great nation, a place where many come. Many hoped to be here and many came from afar to come here. Looking at the past is good 'cause you can learn from your past, see your mistakes and correct them. But, we must move-on to keep building this great nation, fighting for our freedom. Integration is the best thing that ever happened to a people who had a sad and difficult past. I blame the people in the past who had a past and took their anger out on others which in-turn gave them a past ofunhappiness.

-Little Wolf

#89. Donnie: If You Blame People

I thought my life was over. I never thought I would stop drinking and using drugs. Everyday after school, me and 4 other people in our little gang would get "high". And we walked the streets selling drugs and clowning other people, until one day I was stabbed by a rival gang member, next to my heart. He wanted to kill me and he almost did. I was in the hospital for 94 days. And I sat at home for another 68 days. It took a long time to recover from that stabbing, needless to say, I learned my lesson. I grew up with all my boys but I was done with the streets. I went back to school a different person. I want life so much. I was one of those people who have seen the other side of Life and Death and where I went I wouldn't wish it on no one. I was in complete darkness, when I was stabbed, so dark even, I could smell the darkness. It was so thick it weighed me down. I couldn't move. I woke up in the hospital. I was so happy to be alive. I'm doing so good in college and my major is Human Development. I know I want to help others come out of the streets and not go through my experience. If you blame others for your failures you can't see how you really fail.

-Donnie

#90. Hardy

I took my father's gun out of his shoe box and robbed a store for beer and money, 3 friends and I. They wanted to shoot the cashier but I said, "No. Let's take the money and go." One of them said, "But they will see our faces." So we wore Ski masks and we pulled it off. Two days later one of my friends with us was caught with drugs and told on all of us. The police came to the house. My father answered the door and the police arrested me and took his gun for evidence. We were 16 years old. I was in the 10th grade and I did 9 months in jail. After that, my father said to me, "You have a choice: go to school, go back to jail or get out of my house!" I went back to school, I was a changed young man. I know I couldn't make the samemistake twice. I was on probation for 3 years and that was my only chance. What the judge said was: "If you get into any more trouble, you will have gray hair by the time you see day light!" I got a job and started doing good for myself. Afterschool, I worked. I started college and now I'm a businessman. I'm married with 3 kids of my own. My wife owns her own business and my life is wonderful and peaceful. When you blame others, your life becomes a big excuse and you stop using your brain and start using your sorrow and feelings of hate believing that the world is againstyou.

-Hardy

#91. Demore

My life didn't get better until they found my father dead in the streets 6 blocks from where we stay. My mother was devastated from the news. My father used drugs and he owed someone money and they set him up with a "hot shot", bad drugs. Looking after my mother and littlebrothers, Ilearnedresponsibilitysoonafter my father's death. I knew she needed help and selling drugs would not work. So I got a job after school and started working hard helping my mother take care of my brother. I finished high school, started college, dropped-out for a year and then, started back. My life became filled with more and more responsibility to my family and myself. I became a police officer afterdroppingoutofcollegeforthesecondtime and I made enough money to help my mother move into a house and one of my little brothers is also a police officer. And, my other brother plays Pro Football and he's doing very well and so is the family. I know I had to step-up for my family. My mother couldn't do it alone. I stopped blaming my father and started living like a man is supposed to live. I started asking myself, can I help my mother in the ghetto to survive? And I stopped complaining and learned one thing: if you want something done, you must do it yourself. Now who can you blame for that?

-Demore

#92. C. Harty

I'm a girl who wants to go into the Army and my father is against it. "No, No!", he said. "No daughter of mine will serve in the Army!" And as soon as I finished high school, I joined and he was so mad he started drinking more and more. My mother writes me all the time. I asked mama how daddy is doing. I'm the only child. I told them I'm not fighting, I work on a computer and help solve problems with the computers here. I knew my mother wouldn't understand the technical talk of my job, so I keep it simple in my letters. Years have passed, now I am a Captain in the Army, a female Captain. My mother is so proud of me. Daddy is still hurt but okay with his only daughter being a captain.

When I come home, my mother asks me to talk about how well I'm doing and not about his drinking. I did as she asked and I asked my mother if he was going to be okay because now she is dealing with his drinking. My mother is fine, my dad on the other hand is still pouting and he won't say he's proud of me, however I know he is. He wishes I was a boy. He's old school and set in his ways. I have no one but me to blame for my father's drinking but sometimes you have to look-over parents and grow-up.

-Captain C. Harty

#93. Steve

My life didn't start until I was 23 years old after 4 years of college. I looked back on my younger years. How did I make it through high school? I should have been dead. This is how I lived and what I had to die to. My ways were foolish and dumb. I lived on the edge of life everynight, after-school, sellingdrugs, drinking, smoking weed, too tired to go to school the next day. I guess you wonder, "Where are his parents?" My father is in jail, my mother's on drugs and welfare. Having the drugs in the house I feel good, untouchable, but that didn't last long having three little ones under you and mama running the streets. My mother found out that she has Hepatitis-C. Now, she's not doing too good, she's weak all the time. Later, Ihave to choose between my boys or my family. I wanted to live and help with the little ones. I felt sorry for my mother, watching her die slowly, everyday her kidneys were playing out. I started seeking help from the only place I knew: church. Prayers started going up for me and my mother's strength seemed to come from nowhere. I started doing good in school, my grades came up and the will to live and help overwhelmed me. I finished school and college and now I'm a manager for a large clothing store. When you blame others, you realize you are just like them. You can't run nor hide from self.

-Steve

#94. Dennis – Another GangStory

What woke me up is when I was put out in the winter, in the snow, out of my mother and father's house at the age of 17 years old, for disrespecting my mother. I almost froze to death because of my mouth, being bad and tough. I don'tunderstandwhyIwasthe011wayIwasexcept I liked being around the boys and hurting people for the fun of it. After waking up cool for about 4 to 5 months, I went back home and told my mother and father, "I'm ready to be the son I know I can be". I'm not in the gangsanymore. I'm now ready to go to school and learn and get a good education, go to college and finish my degree. I wanted to teach in high school. I thought that's where I belonged, back in school helping troubled kids and showing them the way back home. It took me a long time to love myself again and find myself. I had so much hatred in my spirit and heart. I cared about no one but me for a long time. After finishing high school, I went to college. I worked and my father helped pay for my education. Now I'm in the same school I raised hell in, teaching the kids who remind me of myself and talking to gang members on my own time, changing the course of their lives. I love it and I love myself today. If you blame other people, then it's hard to find yourself and judging them is not helping your future.

-Dennis

#95. Sheila

My parents don't have enough money for me to be what I want to be. My grades are very good, above average, 3.8 is not bad but notgood enough for a scholarship in Law. My hope was one day to be an Attorney-at-Law. My feelings are hurt because I know I can do it. So I decided to work with a law firm. I finished school, went to college, got my degree and worked there for 4 ½ years and they said I was a very bright young lady and asked have I thought of pursuing my education further. I said yes. I could get a scholarship but I know I can be a good attorney and the firm likes me and helped me in school. I finished at 33 years of age. I'm now a lawyer and work with a very nice and beautiful firm. I owe them my life. My careeris very promising and I see myself one day being the best. They told me that I'm here as long as I want to be. Three of the attorneys got together and helped me finish school. I work a little but they understood the time I needed for schooland I worked at that time in the office and at home and when they needed me until I passed the bar. And, they were there for my support every minute. I need them. When you blame others for your low self-esteem, you won't find people to help you nor can people see what's in you and what you really are. If you have high standards you will beaided.

-Sheila

#96. Betty – Nothing Beats a Failure but a Try

Nothing can stop you but you. If you use the word "try" you have already failed. Say, "I will do it" and you will. Not a try but an accomplishment. When you do things, you don't try,

you do it and you completeyoureffortseven if it didn't work for you. You have done your best and the results are what you havedone. This is how we think as talented people and we go after our purpose of being. We must manifest from our highest inner-being what we will be! And not take "I can't" for an answer and failure not for an excuse. There is no such thing as failure, trying and blaming. Ourselves are our problems and our fate is in our hands. Our destinybelongs to ourselves and meditation is good but moving and working toward your goals is also good. We don't want to say down- the-road, "I wish I would have done this or that." No, no. We want to say, "I'm glad I did this in my life. I'm happy to have accomplished my goals and my career is just what I knew it could have been." If you blame anybody but yourself for your failure, you have stopped trying. Never give-up on your dreams. Don't try, just do it.

-Betty

#97. Learning to Give Your All

When I first learned I wasn't giving my all, I asked, what do you mean? I always heard the term, "You can do better than this." I thought it was just an encouraging statement. I don't know. It really means I could do better. I don't know if I could really do much better because I don't know where I was going and what I wanted to be. So I don't know what to give my all to. Not to my little brothers 'cause mother can do that; not my father 'cause mama can do that; not my girlfriend 'cause I don't want to do that, I didn't need to learn to give my all. I had no reason to start. When I became older I wish I would have had practiced more contact with loving people besides my parents andfamily.

My friends was just as lost as I was. As I learned to give me, I thought something was being taken from me. I had to show compassion for those I don't even know? What?! Are you kidding me? Is this learning to give your all? Can I be just a little selfish when it comes to others' feelings? No. Can I be selfish with my love? No. Well, can I be selfish with my fear? No. The reason we give our all is to grow out of fears and selfishness and learn. Giving your all is a humbling experience and a loving adventure.

-This is you remembering to give.

#98. Cause and Effect

Isthisawayoftellingmewhatgoesaround, comes around? Well, this sounds nicer than Karma. Do you reap what you sow? What you put in is what you get out. Do you mean I can't plant tomatoes and expect onions togrow? That's right. What you do in life will be your return? How you treat others is how you will be treated. What you put into education is what you will become and receive. Is life fair? Yes it is, to those who play fair. Your needs and wants have nothing to do with what youdeserve. Your are your best friend or your worst enemy. You are your cause and effect; your hope, your fate, your faith, your abler or enabler. The ones that understand themselves are the first ones to cause good in their lives and not be effected by their own ignorant hand of destruction. If you don'trulesomeoneelse'swill, youmustfeelyour own power of success unstoppable and you will be affected by what you have caused. Knowing yourself, you can see others, we are one, the same things that are in you are in all beings (humans) around you. Be yourself and your gifts and talents willrise.

- I'm just an American. I'm not white, black, yellow nor brown. I'm an American, a human being. I am you.

#99. Loving Yourselves

How can I love others as much as I love myself? How can I want for others as much as I want for myself. I come first at all times. No one comes before me. No one can love me more than I can love myself. If they could, it would have to be a higher love, a love I have not yet felt nor understood. Does such a loveexist? My emotions of what I think of love or what love is only allows me to go so far. Love seems to have it's peak in the physical world. People kill for love but not as much as people in war died. People cry over love but not as much as people die in wars. There are more people who die everyday from accidents than people who cry over love. What is love? It's just an emotion, a feeling, the act of doing for, love is the story of you. A person who loved humans so much. Can we see this in our minds and feel this enormous little spark in us? I only love myself so much and then, anything else would be too exhausting or overdo it. If I love myself too much, how could I feel for others? There would not be any room to give nor to share. Is this possible? Do I share that much ofmyself?

Will there be any of me left? What do you think?

#100. Desires

We must not let our lustful desires interfere with our goals. This energy, desire, has its own intentions. It can overwhelm you and unconsciously break-down the real essential components of your goals. All emotions have their own components of energy and levels they seek. Lustful desires can be very opposing to our real needs. And if we know not to lust, then we shouldn't desire anything we can'tuse for our growth in the person we want to become. If we must desire, we should desire to better ourselves in a humanitarian way and seek a Higher Self for love. The future is not promised to anyone. It's the present, which is awareness, the real growth of our being. We anticipate the future and remember parts of our past but today is here-and-now. We walk in the light of the awareness of our gifts, knowing today is our opportunity to be the best we can be.

What more can you ask for today?

#101. Jean – Overweight

My mother named me Billie Jean after my aunt but I go by "Jean". If they knew my name was Billie, I would be the laughing-stock of the school. Only a few know the Billie-part of my name, the close ones. But I told them if they tell anyone I would never forgive them. So far, so good. But, my name is half the problem. The other half is how I look. I'm short and kinda' fat but cute. I love to eat and smoke weed which makes me eat more than usual. I dress okay. I'm not in a gang, nor have I ever been in a gang, nor have any intentions of joining a gang. They are all around the school and in the school but you're not forced, as I heard about how some people are forced because of where theylive. You can't even walk the streets to go to the store without seeing gangs. But back to my size, I'm a size 18. I want to lose weight and one day I will. Being big is not good in highschool. People talk about you more when you are big but they talk about everybody who's different. And, I'm different. I'm only 5-feet-1 and I weigh about 180 to 185lbs. I'm in the 10th grade. I blame myself for eating too much and smoking weed.

-Jean

Is Jean honest with her problem?
Do you think smoking weed is a part of her
mental low self-esteem?

#102. The Good and The Bad

We are at war! What is this war, right here, where we live? It's a war between the privileged and the have-nots. The wars between the truth and the lies. A war between the people and the leaders, the rich and the poor, the spirit and flesh. Subliminal seduction and the people's freedom to think and know the truth. We must fight for humanity, for truth and justice. Racism is the biggest illusion in the war right here in the United States of America. Segregation is the norm and integration is the key if it is truly integration. We are dealing with a power of darkness which has come in the hearts of the leaders of our country! They have sold their souls for wealth. Mind control is now what is sought to capture the spirits of the American people. Our youth are under a spell. This spell causes the youth to hate, kill and destroy each other without natural affection. They, the Dark Side, create propaganda and spiritual wars, began for the survival of the flesh and for the destruction of spiritual truth. If they can stop you from finding out who you are and your purpose here on Earth, you will not enjoy your true selves, only the illusions of the material plane, which is physical life not spiritual life.

Spiritual life is the souls of humanitarians who know they are spiritual beings in a physical body, not a physical being with a spirit.

#103.

We must learn to see good even in a bad situation. We must learn to accept with humility others' shortcomings and faults. I know being a teen is a life full of fun at that time. No one is asking you to grow-up fast, or stop being a teen in those 7 years of teens but we must grow-up mentally and have fun doing so. We can enjoy our friends and be nice to others who are unfortunate and interact with them. It's easier to help them than to make fun of them. And we can still have fun and be a teen, feeling good about who to help next. We must not be pressured by other teens to be and act like they want us to be, but we must be the person we are called to be. Our inner-self calls us to be different and unique. The energy wespend wanting to be accepted, let's accept our self first. Who we are today and tomorrow will bring us closer to the person we are. Remember that's what they think of you but that's not who you are. So if someone thinks your not "with it", "cool" or "hip", let them spend all that negative energy being wrong about you. You feel right, do right and think right about yourself and the three rights will put you right where you should be going and driving-to.

Right or wrong, what do you think?

#104. Maiya

My name is Maiya. My parents had an airplane accident. The plane crashed. I was so upset, my life, I thought, was over. My aunt had to bring me and my two little brothers in and help take care of us. It's been 2 years now, I'm 16 years old. My two little brothers are 11 and 13 years old. It's hard for us getting used-to not having mom and dad around. I cry all the time. I can't stop thinking about my mother. My aunt is poor. She don't have much money but she helps us as much as she can. It's 3 bedrooms in her apartment. I sleep on the couch. She has kids also. It's hard on me and my brothers. The welfare don't give her much for us, shesaid. She told me one day that she wished she could do more for us but she said, "Get your education. You'll be grown soon. Get you a good job and make your mother and father proud. You know they are watching you". And they are up there. Seven of us in a three bedroom house is too much for me but the only thing that keeps me going is looking out for my littlebrothers'causeit'sdangerouswherewelive and in our school. I miss my mother very much, my father too, but not as much as mom. Why did they have to go? Why were they taken from us when we really needed them? I blame "Him". We need mama anddaddy.

-Maiya

#105. A Story of Two Women

My name is T.J. My mother is in love with another woman. They are always kissing and touching each other. I hate that. I hate seeing my mother like that. I'm 17 years old, this is my last year in school. She's been doing this for about 3 years now. I'm tired of this mess. Some people know about it. I'm embarrassed about her relationship with this person. I don't know what to say to her, how to come to her and tell her I feel this or that. I don't know if she will even listen. Sometimes I don't like going home. I just stay away sometimes even though I'm still nice to her friend. My girlfriend just be trippin' off them. My mom's friend sometimes acts like a man. She wear a lot of pants and men's clothes and she keep her hair cut as short as aman's hair. My father, he hates my mother. He won't come see me there. My little sister, she's only 8 years old, she don't care, she's not by my father, so he doesn't care about her. I'm trying hard to understand what's going on with me. I know I want to leave home as soon as possible. I even thought about selling drugs but they are crazy out there. I'm not a gang member. I blame my mother for hating men. My life could have been better than this.

-T.J.

#106. J. Ray – Another Gang Story

"Life is what you make it", that's what they say. I'm sick of life and what it has made for me. It has made a living hell for me, a life of pain, betrayal and nightmares. Seeing my friends die and go to jail; watching the rapists of my little sister only do 2 years and then get out of jail acting like they haven't done anything; watching my father drink himself to death; watching my mother work hard for a little bit of money. Watch TV, it's all about blacks on the news killing. I'm so tired of life. School is a drag. My grades are D's and F's. I don't care about school, there'stoomuchviolenceinschooland on the streets. I give-up! I think if I can ever get out of this town, I'll never come back. I hate myself. I hate my father and the police because all they do is kill blacks. Chicago schools are bad for people who want to learn. The guys think they are bad, rappers, drug dealers and hustlers. Gangs run my school and teachers are afraid of them. These gangs don't care who they hurt. Some body needs to do something about them. They are sick people with no heart and no feelings for others. I blame the schools for not making it safe to be in school for those who want to learn and can't because it's too much violence, noiseandtoomanyfoolsaroundinthe schools.

-J. Ray

J. Ray blames the schools. Who would you blame?

#107. Benisha – Crack Baby in a Foster Home

My name is Benisha. I stay in a foster home. I'm 14 years old. I always run-away, all thetime. I get tired of being around them, it's about 8 of us. Their rules are "for the birds", I don't follow them. I do what I wanna do, when I wanna do it, that's how I am. My mother makes mesick.

The state took me from her because I was a crack baby, however I don't feel like one. I'm okay. I'm just like other kids but they make me take all these pills for my disorder. I am not dis- ordered. Sometimes, I play like I am, to get my way. Our school is different from the other schools. Now I do admit some of the kids are strange and noisy but I'm not, I'm normal. Sometimes my mother lets me come see her, she's not supposed-to. She found out where I was. My caseworker just so happened to be a friend of the family and she hooked us up. My mother is now in a program getting clean, she has been clean for 9 months and she's now in church. I know I said, "she makes me sick", sometimes I want to be around her but when I turn 18 years old in four years, I might see her more. I hear people talk, they say, "once a drug addict, always a drug addict". I want my mother sometimes in my life. These people are just like me because they get money for you. My mother told me that and she also said she was sorry and that she loves me. I blame her for my life being sad all the time and for me running-away.

-Benisha

Would you blame the mother, the State or yourself?

#108. Stacy

My name is Stacy. What I don't like about school is the teasing and talking about me as if though I'm not right there in front of the one that's doing all the backstabbing, this gets old. People won't just leave other people alone. They act like they got to talk about you or others. The boys are always talking about sex, they are nasty. They always wanna take you to the back halls. I say, "No, we can talk right here." I'm 15 years old. I want to be somebody and something in life. I want to be a nurse or I am going into the Army. I don't use drugs, smoke nor drink like all the others do. Two of the girls I hang- around, sometimes they smoke cigarettes in the girls bathroom, it's always smoky. Sometimes the teachers walk in and ask who'sbeen smoking. They are so dumb, all they have to do is smell the breath of the ones they think are smoking, then they won't have to ask. Most of the time, I like school, I like learning, I like gym and cheerleader practice. And our basketball team is good. I go to a lot of the games but sometimes the gangs are crazy. I blame the police for not controlling the violence of our school's gangs.

-Stacy

Is Stacy any different from the other girls in the other story about gangs, violence in schools and drugs? Growing-up can be tough in different parts of the country but like all the rest of the students in these schools, Stacy has hung- in-there. It's noteasy.

#109. Fred

My mother and father love them some Malcolm X and Martin Luther King Jr. and so did I. I told my mother, I want to do that, talk to people about how other people treat others, 'cause I see it everyday in the ghetto right here where we live. Even the teachers act like they don't want to be around to help kids. They just want their paycheck and that's it. I see this today in my school. All the kids except for a few don't care about school, if they graduate or not. I care because my mother always says, "If you want to be somebody, you have to be different. Be a leader, not a follower and if you can, leadyourselfintogoodcompanyandstayin good company. Be your own man and woman while standing out here in the 'lion's den'. You will accomplish what you will. A humanitarian helping the unlearned and poor people". Even though we were poor, mama and daddy kept pushing us to be better than them and I love them for that. My name is Fred and I blame the education system for not working harder with these kids and me.

-Fre*d*

I like Fred's attitude, do you?

#110. O'dell

When it comes to learning, I think anybody can learn just as well as others. That's if they are not disabled or handicapped. Other people do learn slower than some, that comes from home. Parents not taking time with their kids whentheyareyoung, lettingthemplaytoomuch and not sitting them down at the table and working with them on math, spelling or even getting them sign cards (which would help a lot). I'm so happy my parents worked with me and made me sit at the table with my two brothers. I feel sorry for some of the students in school because they are slow and they just don't get it. I mean, sometimes stuff that's simple for me and others are so hard for them. Sometimes inclassIletthemcopy-offmypaper, Iknow that's what they are doing but I don't say anything. Sometimes I want to help them more butifyouaskthemdotheyneedhelptheymight get mad because it might embarrass them. Or, they might think I think I'm better than them, so I leave them alone. If I was a parent or when I become a parent, I'm going to work with my children and have my wife do the same. The parents just don't know what it's like to be slow in learning, the parents would never know except by looking at the report cards and the grades. Some parents are just as their kids are, slow, having a disorder too, not working with their kids at a young age. I blame the parents for their lack ofattention.

-O'dell

Johnny Richey

Does O'dell have a point? Should parents work more with their children and pay more attention to their study habits? How do you know if a person is slow, if you're not looking or you don't know the signs?

#111. Leroy: I Blame Some People for Blaming Others

When I look around walking to school in the ghettos, I see in my opinion, people young and middle aged that will never be nothin'. Then I see doctors, lawyers, businessmen and women trying to complete school and not letting their dreams be destroyed by their surroundings. I hope their faith in themselves will continue tobe strong and that they don't stop pushing forward to their goals. It's very easy in the ghetto to be discouraged and frustrated because when you look all around you, failure is the norm, they don't call it failure. They call ithustling, getting-paid or some street name of selling- drugs and playing games but I call it giving-up on education and yourselves. The quality of living is frustrating, the housing and the streets are full of violence but to give-up on education to me means you are keeping yourselves in that place where you don't want to be. So why give- up? That's the reason why you've seen what you seen and been through the things you have been through, this should be enough to keep you going and wanting to keep learning, growing toward a "higher self". I do feel some people don't have a choice, some people will never get ahead. And, some of us refuse to think that way. We are the future of America. We are Americans and we arestrong.

Johnny Richey

-Leroy

Leroy is very strong at a young age. He knows where he is going and what it takes to get there. Leroy is now a Sergeant in Law Enforcement.

#112. Tyler

Sometimes I wish I was any color but black because I don't feel treated right. It seems like everybody has a chance but black people. I don't feel like this all the time but if our schools were better I know I could learn. What's stopping me from learning is the people in the schools, they always starting something with others. Why don't they do something about the violence in the schools? I know something can be done. I know it depends where you stay but we live in the ghetto, the people here drop out of school all the time. I don't want to drop out, I want to be somebody. Even though I feel down a lot, I still know that staying in school is the key to being successful in life. Edu:cation is the key and the wayoutofanysituationyourparentsorsociety put you in. You don't have to stay where you are put. America is the land of the free. We are free to go and come as we please in the realms of law. We are poor but we love eachother.

My family is helpful to my education, my parents always say, "You can be somebody!" Who do I blame? I blame myself if I am not free from failure. My parents said, "You are your worst enemy!" And I see this everyday, people killing themselves with drugs and dropping-out of school. The enemy is within.

-Tyler

#113. Irina

I had sex when I was 15 years old in the church bathroom. Nobody knew but me and him. I thought "church" was my middle name. I was there so much. Choir rehearsal, every Wednesday at 5:45 until 7:30, like clockwork for years. But me and him had met for one year and we really liked each other. We dated for6 ½ months and had sex 5 ½ of them. I wasn't allowed to have a boyfriend. My mother and father were very strict on me and my 17year-old brother. Larry, my boyfriend went to a different school, so on Wednesdays I saw him and sometimes my girlfriend. He would come to her house because her mother worked all thetime.

But I could only go over there once a week on Saturdays and we would see each other then. And you know, O yes, I am having a baby boy. I'm almost 16 years old. I'm a junior in high school. I can't finish but I will have my G.E.D. in 18 months. My baby ain't going to stop me from going back to school. I know I need an education out in this world. Mama, daddy, and teachers talk, talk and talk about being somebody. But man! They wouldn't let me go no-where. They was strict on me. I blame them, mama and daddy.

-Irina

How could she have avoided this?

#114. Daijiro

My name is Daijiro. I'm from a family of five, 3 sisters and 1 brother. I'm the oldest. My father worked hard. He was an engineer. My mom watched all of us until we grew up in age, then she opened her own business. Dad doesn't like it but she needed something to do, my mom was very active. When we were growing up, she took us everywhere, including: zoos, museums and movies. In New York I learned people were "cold", everybody for themselves. I learned that at the age of 13 years old. I had to join my people. Talking in the family, to the relatives and friends about what the Americans did to my country, Japan. 85% of them hated America but lived here and didn't want to leave, it's not so much the American people butthe government. I joined a gang in my 'hood. I was bitter and angry. I'm older now but I blame the American government for me getting shot. If it wasn't for them bombing Hiroshima and Nagasaki, my family and friends wouldn't have kept the story of our past in our present, and I live it even now, still, even to this day, watching the killing and violence on movies and DVDs.

I'm still hurt about what happened in Japan, my country and to my people. Who else can I blame but America?

-Daijiro

#115. Sancis

My name is Sancis. I came here in 1982 when I was 15 years old from Chile. I was an exchange student. I was majoring in Law. I started studying hard when I came here. Iheard about "The American Dream", I wanted to be rich at a young age. I love stories about drug lords and rich people. I love to read and learn how they did it. One day in my school and in the restroom I saw some guys smoking. I thought it was just cigarettes but it was a little glass tube, drugs, however I don't know what kind of drugs. I was curious. One of the guys I've seen many times before. They called me over and asked if I wanted to try some. I asked what it was and they told me. I said, "sure" and Ikepttryingthisforabouttwo-and-a-halfyears, off and on. Then I dropped-out of school and started to sell. You probably heard about me if you're from Denver. I'm now doing life in prison because someone tried to rob me and I shot and killed him. I blame the school for not protecting me and not having security like other private schools. I never expected me, myself, to become an addict and a drug dealer. I thought I was forced. I tried the wrong pleasure just to have fun and party, that turned into anightmare. I should have saidno.

-Sancis

#116. Kiki

My name is Kiki. You will never guess what I've been doing. It's one the best kept secrets in any school. Yes, I've been having sex since I was a sophomore. I met this guy in my classroom. He was fine, so fine. I knew he liked me because he would always talk to me after school. We would meet at places no one would see us. He even had a car. I never told no one about me and him because he said, "Nobody has to know who you're with. Not even my friends nor yours. It's none of their business." People talk all the time about other people's business just to be talking. There are haters everywhere you go, you know. I didn't even tell mama and we talk about everything. I kept it from her. She said, "Get aneducation they'll be there." By the time I was in the 12th grade, at the end, I started showing. I wanted this baby 'cause I really loved him. 2 ½ years we were together. He said he would marry me and take care of me and my baby but he don't. My teacher Mr. Comley really disappointed me. Our secret is still a secret, only now a few people know. I'm now 24 years old, I couldn't go to college, I blameMr. Comley for lying to me. Now I work at McDonald's.

-Kiki

#117. Kamilah

Hi, my name is Kamilah. I was walking to school. I met this very nice looking man but he was a lot older than I was. He said he was 19 years old. He asked how old I was. I said 15 ½. I know I looked older 'cause people told me so. I knew he was older than 19 years old but I didn't care. I wanted him but I didn't let him know but I think he knew. I started seeing him after school. My mother started asking questions about my whereabouts. I told her many times that me and the girls stayed after school and practiced with the drill team. She called and found-out I wasn't even considered as a cheerleader on the team. Things got hot and mama started really questioning me. "Where you been"? "Why did you lie"? "What'shis name"? I knew I couldn't tell her the truth, so I made-up a boy my age. Daniel was 27 years old. I found out how old he was but it was too late. I was 16 going on 17 years old. He was only 11 years older than I was. It turned my life upside- down. I was so in love with him and one day just out of the clear blue sky, he disappeared. I never seen him again. I was so hurt, so hurt my mother knew something was wrong. She said, "I told you them boys ain't no good!" I blame Daniel for lying to me and taking advantage of me. Now I know Daniel was a pedophile, he likes younggirls.

-Kamilah

#118. Anthony – About Gangs

Hi I'm 13 years old. Everybody say I rap good. I have a great future in front of me. I'm in the 8th grade. I'm afraid for my life. I don't wanna be in no gang. They say, I have-to, if I want to live. Protection is very important. I asked my dad if I could go to another school. I told him what was going on and they keep messing with me. I told my dad I don't know what to do. He talked to the teachers and other staff and they said, we watch the kids as much as possible for violent behaviors. And if they seethemtheywillbeexpelledfromschool.

There is a No-Tolerance Policy. And that was all. That's it. If I pointed them out they will call me a snitch and problems will start. That's why I don't like school. Besides, they know where I stay. I grew up with them. And the older ones after-school meet them around the corner and get their money. They sell drugs in the school. My father said, "Be A Man! Stand Up To Them!" He had to in school when he was coming-up. My dad, said there'd been gangs for years doing the same thing. I know they have guns because I've seen them and they will shoot you for no reason. My dad don't know how serious this is. I blame him for not understanding the danger he left me in.

-Anthony

What should Anthony do?

#119. Sandra

Hi, my name is Sandra. I'm not that tall. I guess you can call me a midget. It's only 3 of us in this school. People stare at me all the time, I know they be talking about me all the time. I'm not fat but I wish all the time I was taller. It's hard to study in my classes but people are getting used to me and the other two being around. I have 4 years of this humiliation and pressure to want to be accepted and to fit-in. I'm so sad at the time because I see boys I like but it's too embarrassing for them to talk to me. I'm not bad looking, just short. Regardless what I become in life people will see me as different 'cause I'm different. I love myself very much regardless of my difference. I'm sharp too. I'm an "A" student. Sometimes my teachers askme to help others 'cause there's 45 people in our classroom and the teacher can't keep up, so I help. I really feel good helping. When I help, it seems like I'm not judged by others, for me being different. I got to go. This guy I like is calling me. I really hope he knows I'm different from others. Well, we will see. I'm short and pretty. I blame my DNA and my ancestors, I guess that's not so bad. I met him on the Internet, he doesn't know how small I am.

-Sandra

#120. Larry Roy

Me and my sister are twins. One day she was taken from me. I knew something was wrong but I couldn't put my finger on it. What was bothering me? She was my heart, my soul and my best friend. She used to hook me up with her girlfriends. I miss her so much. She died of liver problems at the age of 17. She was so pretty and smart. Everybody liked her. We all miss her. My mother was so sad, so upset. I knew I had to be there for her during this time. I said, "Mama, I'm here. Don't worry, you still have Emily", that's my little sister. She took it so hard, harder than I and her friend. My grandmother came to live with us for awhile.

Mama couldn't work nor eat. Daddy said he never seen her like this. My sister gave me hope. Her death gave me strength, she seems like she was right there with me, gone but still here. I know she's in a better place. She suffered, now it's over. She's at peace. I blame nature, disease, illness and sickness for taking theloveofmylifefrommeataveryyoungage. I'm now Captain Larry Roy at the M. C. P. D.

- Captain Larry Roy

#121. De'Osha

Everybody's is talking on their cellphones in class, in the halls, in the bathrooms, outside, texting, talking and surfing the Internet, this is the normal thing to do. Now what would we do without phones, my iPad, my Internet on my phone and my computer? I'm here at the right time, in the right place. I hear about old-school talk: pencils, erasers, paper and notes. Things are so different now. I'm glad I wasn't born in those days. I like this time I'm in, video games, TV shows, movies, CDs, and video cameras.

We are an advanced people or are we? Is this time a time of overdoing the connection of things technical? Old-School people say we are distracted by technology and images, sound and seduced by falsehood. I don't know about all that, I know I can't learn nor pay attention to teachers, mama and others who say they want to help me 'cause I'm too busy with my earphones. I'm still using my mind to do all that, so what's the problem? We just got it easier than the '50s, '60s, '70s, '80s, '90s, and 2000s. We are different. We learn differently and we learn quicker because of the reservoir of energy and knowledge that is obtained by the technology that's here now! I'm De'Osha and I'm a Tech Wiz. I'm good. I blame you for not being in this time.

-De'Osha

#122. I Am You

What's up? Hey, they say I'm funny. I like telling stories. People say, "You'll be comedian, some funny person on TV." I'm serious, they really believe this. I like telling jokes. I like watching people laugh. I get energy from that. It makes me even more funny. I can really clown with 6 or 7 people standing around listening. Do you need a good education to go into comedy? I say yes because you have to learn how to manage your money. Yes, it's important as being a doctor, lawyer, judge, District Attorney (D.A.), police officer oretc.

You can have one of these prestigious jobs with an education. Natural gifts are just as important. You need to know many things can be accomplished by the energy of disciplining and nurturing talent but both have to be directed and earned. Everybody has a story but very few hear their calling: that voice that's deep in you whispering, keep going, don't give-up, you can doit!
Listen, listen and hear what you are or what you want to be. I'm you, I'm an American who dreamed the dream, who listened and heard the whisper. I thank friends and you for believing in me and yourselves, never stopping, never doubting and alwaysgrateful.

-You

#123. P. J.

I'm the last one to talk to you. I'm P. J. Everything I say you read, you think is new, it's not. It's been happening for years. I've been there. I'm 73 years old. Before I tell you what I was, Let's start with: love for yourselves and others is very important and very disappointing for the hearts and spirits of you who read how others feel or think and become one of them.

We are all Americans, we are sisters and brothers, children and grandchildren, protecting each other. A million good souls are better than the hearts of the divided on Earth, and they are many more. The Americans have always led by honesty and hope and love, that's who we are and that's what we stand for. That's who you are. A great loving and loved human being. The proud and the brave, whatever you putyour mind to you can achieve. I was just like you, I was from the ghetto, from the suburbs, middle-class, a drug-addict, a rape victim, singleparent, suffering death, disappointment and stress. But I made it. I became what I wanted to be and lived it. There's no reason why you can't do it. You know the story and what it takes to get there. I've been married for 26 years, have 9 grandkids, a good husband, 3 children and I'm a Professor ofLaw!

-P. J.

#124. Brenz

You never know who you're talking to in school, there's some strange people. My name is Brenz. And boy, to-you-from-me, I have something to tell you! Some of the girls in two schools came up missing. Now check this out, 3 girls were found in different places, 2 from our school and 1 from the school about 3 ½ miles away. Well, what do you think happened?

Your typical news about these schools? No that's not it. I knew this weird dude (guy). I seen him everyday, he was a 12th grader. I'm in the 10th grade. When I heard what he did, I was not surprised. He looked like he could have done that. People were so concerned about their schools after the news hit-the-streets. One of the girls was his girlfriend and the coldthing about it was: all three girls knew each other. He killed all three. I was so upset with this school. How could they let this happen? A psycho' killerattheageof18yearsold, youwouldnever know who's who, what a person is thinking, what's in their mind and their little secrets. In 2 weeks people forgot about this and went on with their lives. I never stop thinking of it. I'm blaming this school and the other school for not seeing and observing this. Why couldn't they have been more proactive? Who cares about the poor? Noone.

-Brenz

#125. Carrie

Hi my name is Carrie. I'm a "B" Student. I'm pretty smart. I like boys but I don't want to go out with any boy yet, not until I'm in the 11th or 12th grade. Something happened to me and it seems like the whole school knew about my little secret. I went over to the house of a friend of mine and we were talking and two more of his friends came over, plus another girl I'd never seen. I ended up having a drink with them and before you knew it, I was pretty tipsy. I was there about 3 – 4 hours. I don't know what happened between those hours. Something was put in my drink and they had their way with me. The other girl was with one of the guys. They took pictures of me with no clothes on with a drink in my hand and a hat on my head. This ended up on all of their friends' phones and on Facebook. I'm not that kind of girl. Why would they do that to me? That's not right. I never did anything with them willingly, they tricked me. I was too embarrassed to go to any teachers and my parents and tell them about this. I blame these boys for being so mean to me. They didn't have to do that to me nor should anyone have to go through that kind of embarrassment.

-Carrie

#126. Rosella

My son was only 7 ½ months old when he died. My mother was watching him while I was in school. I was so broken, so sad, I dropped out of school, and I told my mother she should have kept a closer eye on my baby. If I was there it wouldn't have happened. I would have been playing with him, feeding and holding him not just leaving my baby in the room in the bed entertaining my boyfriends. All the other kids were in school. My little sister is 12 and my brother is 9 years old. So, my mother had no excuse for not watching my baby while I was at school, just like she used to leave us when I was small or young. I think she did the same thing with my baby. I think she left and went somewhere with her friend and when she came home, he was dead. When he needed her, his grandmother, she wasn't there for him. The people called it "Crib Death" but I know better. I said I'll never speak to her again for being irresponsible watching my baby. I'm now 26 years old. My little brother and sister, I haven't seen in almost 10 years. I moved out of state. I hitched a ride all the way to L. A. (Los Angeles) from Detroit, Michigan. I blame my mother for my baby's death and for not being able to seemy little brother andsister.

-Rosella

Should Rosella blame her mother? What about Rosella getting pregnant in-the-first-place? Who does she blame for that? How can she blame her mother for not seeing her brother and sister while she's the one that left?

#127. Shanoshia

My mother and father were Jehovah's Witnesses. Birthdays and holidays were the most miserable times in our lives, especially during Christmas. All the lights and singing during this time made my brothers and sisters sad, very unhappy. We got no prizes, no trees in the house; no Thanksgiving; no Halloween; no 4th of July, no Easter; not even a birthdaygift.

We knew how old we were, that's it. Every Saturday, we would go to the Hall and worship. I wanted out so bad 'cause I didn't believe like my parents believed. I wanted to be a child, a little girl and a person that thinks on their own. My parents decided everything in our lives for us, even when I was 17 years old. I'm next to the youngest out of 5 children, 3 are gone, they got out of my parents house as soon as possible. When I'm 18 years old, I'm out too. My children will have birthday parties, Halloween, Costumes, Thanksgiving Dinner, Christmas Gifts, Easter Clothes and Bar-B-Q for the 4th of July. I will not live like my parents live.

Children should have a choice at a certain age as they grow and mature they should have some kind of say so over their activities in school and outside of school, my name is Shanoshia. I blame my parents for being too religious and perfect.

-Shanoshia

#128. Penny

Everywhere you look on TV, billboards, magazines, books, Reader's Digest and etc., you see women, girls, ladies, females advertising a product. It really makes no difference what they're advertising: dog food, coffee, clothes, batteries, soap or salad, females are doing it. As we grow up to be ladies, commercials help pave the way being a female. It's part of society.

Even little girls, 7, 8, 12 grow-up with a little boost in their sexuality because of TV advertising, websites and video games. You name it and it's out there for them to see even if parents monitor what's heard, seen or talked- about, sexuality is there right in front of their eyes. Kids will listen and see what you can't control, parents are three steps behind. 80% of parents can stop what their kids see and hear. As kids grow up into teen-hood, they are ready for what they have learned from childhood and #1 is sexuality. Do we still wonder why teen pregnancy is on the rise? I'm Penny and I'm pregnant. I'm 15 years old. TV made me feel like a little lady. Websites, magazines and advertisements are a conscious effort to seduce the consumer. I blame all of them for seducing Americans, including children.

-Penny

Does Penny make a good point about whom she's blaming?

#129. Niki

Hi my name is Niki. I think I was 7 ½ years old when I was awakened from sleep, when I heard yelling in the living room. I thought it was my mother and father arguing again but it was another man in the house screaming at my father saying, "Man! Where is my money?

Where is it?" Soon after that I heard two shots, I was so afraid I thought someone shot my dad. Mother was screaming. I got up out of my bed, went to my mother, stood by her and my father was standing over this man. Soon after, they came and took the man off the floor and my father was taken to jail. I was 27 years old when I saw my father again. School was hard for me, from there on. My father was nice to me, I was the oldest out of three. My life changedfrom there on. I turned out to become a numbers-runner, gambling at the age of 12. I dropped out of school. I blame my father.

-Niki

#130. Lee Lee

My name is Lee Lee. I was born deformed. My wrist curls-up, I can't straighten my fingers. They call me "Chicken Wing", that's my nickname. All the time, I'm teased continually in-class and out-of-class. I can't play sports and I love sports. Basketball is my favorite game. I wish all the time I was normal like other kids. I have no girlfriend. This one girl likes me but she has a short leg. She was also born deformed. Why do I have to be like this? Why does she have to be the way she is? Why did our parents use when we were growing inside? Why didn't they care enough and understand they were hurting us? She also said her mother used too. We are the results of drug use in early pregnancy. And during the time wemost needed nourishment, we got drugs instead of what we needed from them. I feel sorry for her too. There are so many of us here in this school who have drug-addicted parents. In turn we are the result of their drugs. I blame drug-dealers and my mother and the other kids' parents. I'm now 21 years old. I still have hatred towards drug-dealers.

-Lee Lee

#131. Rayshawn

My mother and father are so different from others. What I mean is, they follow their jobs from town-to-town, city-to-city, and state-to- state. I never really get to know people like others, to spend time with each other, girls I liked, friends I had. Now, I'll never see them again. I am now in this school, mostly Hispanic, 75%. I'm black and I'm so uncomfortable around them. I know they are talking about me and my sister. They don't even talk tous.

Sometimes a few say, "Hi". We feel out of place, my sister and I. My parents' excuse is that, "We can learn Spanish" while we're here. Most classes are in English, so there's not a problem learning. My sister and I eat together at schoolallthetimeandcomehometogethertoo. Everywhere you go, there's gangs and they don't like us. The good thing about our safety is that we walk home also with a few associates. I can't call them friends, not yet, but their presence helps to keep my sister and I safe. I told my parents about this and they said they looked into the area we stay in and it's safe. I blame them for moving all the time and if anything happens to my little sister, I'll never forgivethem.

African-American should be in African- American schools.

-Rayshawn

#132 .Mohammed

I'm Mohammed. I was born here in America.

I was in the 9th grade when the Twin Towers came down. I caught hell. A few of us who were from the Middle East we were called names, "Children of Terrorists", "Sand- Monkey" and "Bin Laden". They were so mean to us, it's only a few of us in school. My parents, who are Americans, not Arabs are good American tax payers but we missed 6 weeks of school because of what others had done. And, we were picked-on and treated very bad. My parents thought it would be best for me to take a break from school until thingscooled-down.

The teachers and staff thought it would also be best 'cause they couldn't watch all the other students at once. And, there were many sad people during that time. But I didn't do anything to anyone but I became their enemy because of others' fighting and hatred. I blame my people and the American Government and the Jewish people for fighting the Arab Nations also.

-Mohammed

#133.

Hi, I'm a Black Man, a White Man, an East Indian, a Hispanic, a Jewish Man, a Japanese, a Chinese. I'm a Young American who is sick n' tired of racism, of gangs, of corporate greed, the government, how people are being treated, of religion, of cults, I'm just sick of it all. People are people, the Children of the Universe, the Children of the Earth. Why can't we see this?

Why do we fight each other continually for power, food, money and social order? We are so divided and we are supposed to be Americans: "The Great Melting Pot People of Earth" and we have melted into division, many of them different species of beasts whorun-after greed and material gain, not caring at all about the poor nor the sick not domesticallynor internationally. I blame you, you and you too for not standing-up as real humanitarian Americans and for accepting the illusion of peace, love and equality.

#134. Adat

Hi, my name is Adat. I am from Ghana, West Africa. I'm very dark-skinned, darker than most. They call me "Midnight". I'm not so different from others, just darker. Here in America, people are cruel, mean and always lookingfor fights, challenging each other for the silliest of things I've ever seen. In Africa we're not like this, we are one, like it should be. My health is your health. My spirit is yours. We are one in hunger, poverty and in looks. But there are some people who don't want oneness, they want individuality because they don't want to share their love, peace and happiness. They are selfish individuals who want to challenge life's harmony, its nature, upsetting life's order. We are all human beings working together forone goal: to protect, love and cherish each other's individualities to become one in likeness. That likeness is, being a loving, sharing, forgiving human being. I blame segregation and others who have an "inferiority complex" about themselves and others.

-Adat

#135. Hi, I am You

Hi, I'm you. Fear I was told is our enemy, our expectation of failure. We have so many fears. Fear overwhelms us and takes us to its own hellish place. And it locks us in its rooms of insecurities, a box that's too high and hard to climb out-of. Walking in fear is wrong for those who want to achieve greatness. I'm not saying be foolish and don't protect yourselves, yes there are dangers, in our communities, schools, in some of our homes, but fear is everywhere. It endangers your future, your ability to become what you are capable of being. It interferes with your courage, your guts, your map to success. It is fear that masks itself to those who have low self-esteem. It was fear that people had in the past who assassinated great teachersbecause they didn't want change. Fear causes segregation in the hearts of those who can't change and don't want others to change. Let us conquer fear and blame no one but our hearts for not helping others who are in fear and let us not assassinate their characters. We are Americans: A GreatPeople.

- You

#136. Emily - "We Are Americans"

We are a strong people, a loved people and a peaceful people. The Americans are an intelligent people who lead the world in many different things. Our great leaders gave their lives for this country for it to become what it is today. America gives you the chance to be what you want to be. America is a place where everyone is coming to for freedom, liberty and justice for all who live here. We are friends to the people of this Earth and to one another aswe stand for liberty and freedom. America is not a perfect place but it is better than most. I would rather be here than any other place on Earth. I see so much about other countries. It's sad to see people suffering hunger, thirst, disease and sickness striking the poor. I'm not poor norrich. I'm happyto be here, born here, living right here in America. My name is Emily, I'm 11 years old. I thank my parents for being Americans 'cause I could have been born to a very, very poor family in a poorcountry.

-Emily

#137. Jean – Adoption Story

He raped me too many times and I got tired of him touching me at night while I was trying to sleep. I really got sick of him, my foster father. I told my foster mother and she slapped me in the face hard and said to me, "Don't you never let me hear you talk like that in my house ever, never again! Joe is a good man and you are a liar! And, I will call the state and have them come and get you and we will see who believes your lies!" She called me a little black b. I'm 13 years old, I said, I'm sorry mama. She said, "Don't you call me mama until yougotellJoeyou'resorryforallyourlies!"and I said, yes ma'am. Mama worked at night, she would come home about 12:30 or 1:00 AM and he would be done by then back in hisroom sleep. I went to school the next day feeling sad, dirty and violated. I don't know who to tell. My teacher asked me, "Baby what's wrong? You can tell me. It will be our secret". I told her.

They had me checked and he was placed under arrest. By now mama hated me and I was placed in another home and she was black and I remembered her giving me the house rules and the do-s and don't-s. I knew I would like this home. She had a daughter my age, my teacher knew her, my teacher helped me and today I'm so happy. I blame the state for not looking more into families' histories who adoptchildren.

-Jean

Jean knew who to tell. A teacher, a police officer, a mail man, a woman, a friend of the family can always help.

#138. Hispanic Americans

I'm Juan. I love America. I love the people, the work, the freedom, the schools, the laws and the institutions which carry America to leadership. I'm so happy to be an American.

How can people complain, worry and hate? They see their opportunity to be what they want and can be in such a great nation; a place that gives you the freedom you need to be complete in your self, to rise to any occupation you want to be. I ask myself: who am I? What can I do to make a difference in my life and in others' lives? However, we must love ourselves first and to do so, we must listen to what we are and how we can get there, to be that person of integrity responsible for our feelings and living conditions. Who would you blame if you were me?

-Juan.

#139. Norman – Another Gang Story

I have low self-esteem, I just knew I wouldn't make-it. I knew it was no way I would finish high school and go to college. I was in the gangs in the streets and my best friend was killed. I never got arrested for any of my crimes. I was never caught. I learned anotherway.

First, church, being around positive people; I changed schools with my father's "Okay" and started my new life. My mother and father were church members, my grades started picking-up. I got into school activities and sports. I learned I had submitted to my lower-self and I had given- up but since my new life began, I found one thing in me to be true: that if I put my mind to anything, I will do it, I will finish what I started. My lower self was silly and dangerous moreto myself than others. I put myself in harm's way more than gangs did. It was me, all my doing, now I'm in college. It's been two years, I'm doing very good, I have good study habits and my major is films. I want to be a director of movies and I know I will do this and be that which I have started to be. My story is: if you blamepeopleforyourfailure, howcanyoulearn from your ownmistakes?

-Norman

What does Norman mean by the term "lower self"?

#140. Jewish Americans

Our people went through hell and back. I wouldn't trade who I am today for nothing and nobody. I'm an American. I feel free and equal to any other. I'm just as good as anyone on Earth. America is a place I honor and respect, a great nation to be in. Proud people, good people and happy people are successful people loving a place where you can feel loved, seeing you are protected from your enemies and loved by your friends. When we want a change, we get it 'cause we are the people who give changes.

When something goes wrong, we are the people who make it right. When the hungry need food, we provide. We are educated and taught by each other; we support one another; help each other and fight alongside each otheragainst others. Yes I blame Hitler and their evil but I have forgiven him for his ignorant insanity.

-Jeremiah

#141. Mercy

I was adopted. I'm brown-skinned and my mother and father are white but they are poor just like people of all colors in the ghetto. My parents catch hell everyday. They are called names, white this and white that. It's very bad, they have been robbed many, many times and beaten-up. My mother and father really love me but I'm black. Why did they adopt me? Why not their own? I love them too, but sometimes I getembarrassedwalkingwiththemamongallof these black people. They call me, "Uncle Tom's Little Girl". They laugh at me, make fun of me all the time but there are a few white familieswe stay around. I'm not the only black female nor male adopted into white families. White people are also good people. And some just likeblacks, Spanish and many other races or nationalities have good and bad behaviors. I can't help but to think that blacks have become very racist like white people. It's very sad the way they are treated and how their ancestors were treated and you can't blame them. Blacks are more homeless than any other race in America and I know this because of their history and the ways of the American government and their willingness to mistreat people. I go through hell in school. I blame racism for all of this division andhatred.

-Mercy

How do you think Mercy really feels about being adopted by a white family as she grows- up and starts to understand and identify with her culture?

#142. All Americans

All Americans are waking up to just being an American. They are saying, "Enough is enough! Let's grow together, build together, sell and work together." We can and will live together while we are here on Earth, watching one another grow old together, delivering our children together, watching our elders together, the one's that taught us to be men and women, those who made and paved the way to equality, justice and freedom for us all. Great respect is given and is deserved for our elders. We weren't here to fight, we came after the fight, we weren't here when the train tracks were laid but we ride on the trains. This is America, The Greatest Nation on Earth. We welcome you and get you started for your greatness inour institutions of learning. You go out and share and give back what was given to you: freedom, justice, peace, love and equality.

#143. Sharon - A Ghetto Story

I feel like a prisoner in jail in my 'hood, this ghetto. I want out of this place so bad, I wish there wasn't no such thing as the ghetto and people can live where they want to, poor or rich. I'm sick of this place, all the killing and fighting. I pray, I pray to God to free me from this prison. Going to school is just another part of this big prison. In the street when I look around me people are so sad here, so depressed, angry with themselves and others. They take their anger out on others in the schools, the streets, the churches and even at home. Violence everywhere. No peace, no love, no faith, no hope, no money. And no fun in school like school is supposed to be, peaceful and hopeful for the futures to come. But I know not my school. Gangs fighting, teachers talking to girls for sex and drugs, 15 to 18 year olds looking like they are 21 to 25 year old ladies (or women). This place is a trip! This ghetto, I have to get out of it before I die. People will put you into some mess because they are not happy here and I can't blame them. It's a nightmare, an accident waiting to happen, a bomb waiting to explode. I blame the government.

-Sharon

Is the ghetto that bad? Is there a way out of these conditions?

#144. Carolyn

As my uncle raped me over and over again, I started to become numb, I started not to care.

Go ahead, I said to myself. All the threats of hurting me, if I were to tell anyone about what he's doing to me took a toll on me. One day, my girlfriend Day-Day asked me was he still doing that to me. I said yes. She said, "tell someone". I said, I couldn't. My friend had told her teacher and I was called to the Principal's Office and a Police Officer was there. I had to tell itall.

Thanks to my best friend my nightmare was over. My uncle was put in jail and away from me for 15 years. I was 11 years old during this time. I blame my mother for not watching her brother.

-Carolyn

Carolyn's best friend Day-Day found the courage to help her friend. If your friend told you a secret like that, would you tell if you knew she would not get into trouble?

#145. Seeing Your Own Reflection While You Create

As you create good things in your life, you can see it and feel it. Happiness is the feeling you feel. Seeing it is being around positive and loving people. You know you are doing something right, thinking healthy and right. But this is not so when you are influenced by the wrong thoughts of your friends and yourself.

We see our reflection from our own hands, what we think makes a big difference in our lives, where we are headed and where we arrive. We must see ourselves in the future as happy, mature men and women 'cause one day that's what we will become – Men and Women. So, how we think now will have a lot to do with our future and right now, we begin to think healthy thoughts, have healthy friends with common goals who reflect beauty.

Final Wisdom

Active Behavioral Conduct Disciplines©
by Thomas Boothe ©1979

Wisdom only comes from two sources, instinct and experience. Never allow anxiousness, selfishness and greed to consume your instinct and experience. In the absence of wisdom lay foolishness, regret and despair to remember.

Final Wisdom

1. Remember to think before speaking.
2. Remember to think before doing.
3. Remember to give the other person the benefit of the doubt, especially when strong feelings are involved.
4. Remember that when given the same history, timing, circumstances and situation, you could have been that other unreasonable, selfish person who confronted you unfairly
5. Remember to look for the fact and truth of the matter.
6. Remember to try and win the person, not the argument.
7. Remember that all things have at least two sides, but no one has enough wisdom to see them all.
8. Remember that respect precludes prejudices of all kinds toward others and wards off vexation of spirit, mind and body.
9. Remember that the reality of your life will become more valuable with age.
10. Remember that there are only two entities that are fundamental to reality: they are communication and transportation (influence and motion).
11. Remember that reality must equal the knowledge of actual experience to your senses: energy to energy, matter to matter, substance to substance. Thoughts and beliefs do not have these qualities.
12. Remember that your life has only the value you place on it at any given time.
13. Remember that money does not buy truth.

14. Remember that no person or thing planned their time or place to be born or created.
15. Remember that the most any person can be responsible for giving is their best effort, if it is truly their best effort.
16. Remember that life's forces have no favorites: it provides a living environment for all, from the amoeba to humans.
17. Remember that each living being instinctively knows its needs, but has no control over the forces that provides them, each are dependent on the other.
18. Remember that compassion is a human asset if used unselfishly, but a liability otherwise.
19. Remember that miscommunication is far worse than no communication.
20. Remember that consistency is the key to success in any relationship
21. Remember that each of us has a purpose and a small part of that purpose is to know what that purpose is, the rest is performance.

The wisdom of opportunity is preparation.
Opportunities will only benefit those who are
prepared to perform.

Boothe Protocol for Determining Ongoing Success

Determinant No.1 – Decisions and Choices; Choices and Decisions
All things depend upon the wisdom to make the right decision and choice at the right time.

Determinant No. 2 – Selections
Choices are acted upon: Who? What? Where? When? How? And Why?

Determinant No. 3 – Preparation
Success is always effected by how well a person is prepared to perform the task at hand.

Determinant No. 4 – Dedication
Success is equally effected by the amount of dedication, determination and passion connected from the person to the task at hand.

Determinant No. 5 – Follow-through
Success is finally effected by follow-through in completing the task at hand

Determinant No. 6 – Standardization

Ongoing Success is effected by whether a person standardizes his or her performances so they can be repeated with the same results over and over again. (The mark of winners and especially of champions.)

Temper actions with a smile, style, substance and skill.
Make humility and humor a part of all relationships.

www.ingramcontent.com/pod-product-compliance
Lightning Source LLC
LaVergne TN
LVHW091047100526
838202LV00077B/3065